Jungle Thorn

Dear Lisa,

I hope you'll enjoy and be closer to Jesus as you read / listen this story!

Happy birthday !!!

Love, Samantha & Omar

Weimar, 10/15/16

Kondima in front of her Borneo home.

Jungle Thorn

By
Norma R. Youngberg

*Illustrated by
Harold W. Nunson*

TEACH Services, Inc.
PUBLISHING
www.TEACHServices.com • (800) 367-1844

World rights reserved. This book or any portion thereof may not be copied or reproduced in any form or manner whatever, except as provided by law, without the written permission of the publisher, except by a reviewer who may quote brief passages in a review.

This book was written to provide truthful information in regard to the subject matter covered. The author assumes full responsibility for the accuracy of all facts and quotations as cited in this book. The opinions expressed in this book are the author's personal views and interpretation of the Bible, Spirit of Prophecy, and/or contemporary authors and do not necessarily reflect those of TEACH Services, Inc.

This book is sold with the understanding that the publisher is not engaged in giving spiritual, legal, medical, or other professional advice. If authoritative advice is needed, the reader should seek the counsel of a competent professional.

Copyright © 2000, Revised 2013 TEACH Services, Inc.

ISBN-13: 978-1-57258-157-9 (Paperback)
ISBN-13: 978-1-57258-979-7 (ePub)
ISBN-13: 978-1-4796-0071-7 (Kindle/Mobi)
Library of Congress Control Number: 99-6813

Published by

www.TEACHServices.com • (800) 367-1844

Contents

Preface.. viii

Chapter One   Jungle Thorn 9

Chapter Two   Tuan Makes A Proposition 19

Chapter Three   King Of The Centipedes.....................27

Chapter Four   The Answer Is Yes 39

Chapter Five   Beyond The Blue Mountain 49

Chapter Six   The House Of Children 59

Chapter Seven   The Valley Of Water.............................71

Chapter Eight   The House Of Sickness 81

Chapter Nine   Into The Sunrise 91

Chapter Ten   Magic Beyond Magic 101

Chapter Eleven   Lost And Found 109

Chapter Twelve   The Pigs That Preached The Gospel................. 119

Preface

The life and ministry of a great missionary is often best revealed by a simple story, a single incident, a particular happening.

In the story of Kondima I have tried to paint a close-up picture of a missionary at work and to show how he fits into the need of the jungle folk.

That the truly loving heart will find ready response in any land among any people; that, underneath, the feelings of the whole world are alike; and that the mission work in the faraway places is worth while—these are the messages I have committed to *Jungle Thorn.* I trust that you will receive them and enjoy them.

—Norma R. Youngberg

Chapter One

Jungle Thorn

"I think when I read that sweet story of old,
When Jesus was here among men,
How He called little children as lambs to His fold.
I should like to have been with them then."

"KONDIMA, oh, Kondima," chirped Mookit's shrill voice, "come with us to hunt mushrooms." A tousled head appeared in the door as a brown-faced boy of seven years mounted the steep ladder which furnished entrance to the stilted hut on the Borneo mountainside.

Kondima had been struggling with some small strips of bamboo, trying, with a few directions from Mother, to turn the wriggling things into a basket. It was tedious work, and she was glad to leave; so at the sound of Mookit's voice she sprang to her feet and snatched up a basket from the corner near the stove. Leaving Mother to pick up the unfinished basket, she hurried down the ladder with her little friend.

"Really, truly, are there mushrooms?" questioned Kondima as she joined the group of four village children,"Yes, oh, yes," cried Alijah, "right up at the edge of the big woods on the hill. We found a whole basketful just now, and there are lots more."

The children trooped up the hill to the edge of the jungle. Sure

Above: Kondima looks at her eye as it is reflected in the pool.
Below: The Tuan *(missionary)* visits Kondima's people.

enough, the fat mushrooms were just poking their shiny, bulging tops through the soft, damp earth. The children ran here and there shouting to one another and pointing out more and more of the big white mushrooms.

The sun had been low in the heavens when they began their expedition; and because they knew that it would soon fade behind the green mountain and the early darkness would fall, they worked fast. Before long each child had what he considered an ample supply of the tender mushrooms for the use of his family. Still the sun hung like a ball of fire over the mountain across the valley.

"Let's have a monkey game," shouted Mookit. At once all the children leaped into the edge of the jungle and began swinging on the long creepers that hung from the great trees.

"If I had Father's jungle knife, sang Mookit from his lofty perch, "I could cut a path into that brush. It's too bad we can't get back to that big ironwood tree. Look at the rattan vine hanging clear from the top." All the children looked.

"We can't swing on rattan vines," Kondima said as she swayed and tossed on a slender creeper. "Those vines have big thorns."

When the little ones had played at swinging for a few minutes, a strange noise deep in the forest startled them. Fearful that some wild animal might be close at hand, they all scrambled through the tangled vines and back to where they had left their baskets.

Kondima had chosen a very slender vine for her swing, and in her fright she gave it a hard jerk. It broke, and she was thrown deep into the thicket. A sharp pain stabbed her eye. She heard the children calling, "Kondima, where are you?"

Heavy sobs shook her small body, but in terrible fear she kept struggling through the thick vines in the direction of the friendly voices.

Jungle Thorn

"I just bet a *gee-ok* stung her," volunteered Mookit; "those white-looking ones sting like fire." He pointed to a fuzzy, pinkish-white caterpillar clinging to the bark of a sapling.

"Never mind the *gee-ok*, Kondima; come put mud on it, and it won't hurt so much." At this moment Kondima emerged from the jungle holding one hand over her right eye and sobbing convulsively.

Mookit ran to her. "Let's see the hurt," he urged sympathetically, trying to pull the hand away. For an answer, Kondima gave him a hard kick on the knee, held her hand tighter over her eye, and cried louder and louder.

Mookit picked up Kondima's basket of mushrooms as well as his own. All the children trotted down the hill. Kondima followed as fast as she could. Her sobs had increased to loud wailing, and the wailing now became shrill screams.

"Child, child, what is the matter?" Mother came running with Baby Bani on her back. At the sound of Mother's voice Kondima just sank down on the ground. The small legs refused to go any farther. Mother drew the little brown hand away. "Adoh, Adoh! Look, oh, look! A great thorn has gone clear into her eye!" She screamed as loudly as the child, and presently all the women came running to see what was wrong.

"It has broken right off so it can't be drawn out," exclaimed Kokit's daughter, bending over the child. This graceful young woman was a person of action, and she untied Baby Bani from Mother's back, handing him to one of his aunties for safekeeping.

Kondima was a big girl, six years old; but the mother lifted her easily and carried her to the spring where clear, cool water trickled from a bamboo trough. There she washed the injured eye over and over again. The cool water revived the fainting little one, and she began to scream with renewed energy.

Jungle Thorn

"What goes on here?" questioned a gruff voice.

Kondima's father had just returned from harvesting in a distant clearing and knew nothing of the accident. A dozen voices began a loud explanation. He elbowed his way through them all and took his little daughter in his arms.

Comforted by the security of her father's strong arms, Kondima ventured to open her left eye just a little, but the look in Father's face caused her to scream with redoubled vigor. She had never seen her father look so grave.

"It must be taken out," Father said through clenched teeth. "It must be taken out, but I can't see how."

No one in all the crowd now assembled could give a single suggestion, but Kokit's daughter ventured the opinion that "her eye will never be any good any more anyhow." All these things fell like a rain of suffering on the heart of Kondima.

Throughout that night Father held the tossing child. With many words of love and comfort he tried to soothe her, but she did not sleep or eat for many days. She drank water from the spring in large, long draughts, for her small body was hot with fever.

Finally through the natural process of the decay of injured tissues, the heavy thorn came away; but Kondima sensed that her eye was a pitiful, repulsive sight.

As the weeks went by, the little girl ran about the village again, but not with her former carefree abandon. The left eye was sore and red out of sympathy with the ruined right eye. Kondima had no looking glass, but the clear pool at the spring taught her many things.

"Chaya," called Mother one day several weeks later, "go to the teacher's house and ask him when the white *Tuan* [missionary] will come."

Since Kondima's sad accident Chaya had been sent on all the errands.

"Do they feel ashamed of me, I wonder," thought little Kondima as without any protest she watched Chaya go.

"My poor eye is worse to look at every day," she spoke with quivering lips. "Nobody wants to look at me any more. Chaya must do all the interesting things; she must even go to inquire about the *Tuan*." Saying this, she crawled into a dark corner by the clay stove.

Chaya returned presently with the news that *Tuan* would be coming to Durian village that very evening.

"Come, then," said Mother, "we will prepare rice cakes. We must have food to set before the *Tuan* after his long journey up the mountain."

The visits of the missionary were great occasions in the mountain village. He did not come often, but when he came, he always brought something good and interesting. Sometimes he brought bright pictures which the children could fasten to the walls of their bamboo huts. Always he brought medicine for fevers and stomach-aches. He also brought instruments for pulling teeth. He was often busy for hours taking the aching teeth from the mouths of the patient villagers.

Jungle Thorn

The children knew that in the big pockets of his khaki coat were bits of bright candy. He knew and loved them all. Yes, it was a great day when *Tuan* came to the village.

Blind old Kokit, who suffered from constant aches and pains, waited for the *Tuan* to come and bring his hot "rubbing medicine." "I can feel the devils going out of my bones when the *Tuan* puts his hands on me," the old man grunted. He was still a heathen; in fact, the village was about evenly divided between the old heathen ways and the new teaching about Jesus that had come to Durian village a few years before. Nevertheless, when the *Tuan* came, all alike welcomed him with joy. The blessings he and his teachers brought were for all.

Kondima had always been a great favorite with the *Tuan*. Now, with a sad little heart, she watched her mother and Chaya preparing the cakes. "He won't remember me," she said over and over to herself.

She was just crawling off to cry when Mother called her. "Kondima, you help us weave the little cake baskets."

She sat down beside Chaya on the split bamboo floor and drew a pile of green leaves toward her. With willing fingers she plaited the four long strips of green into a tight little box, perfectly woven together with a long tail of green leaf to hold it by. It could be opened just a little so the washed rice could be poured in. Chaya put just the right amount into each little basket box. Mother had a big kettle of boiling water ready. The little green boxes were fastened together in clusters by their long "tails" and boiled in the kettle until the rice swelled up and filled each little container to a state of perfection. This did not take long. When the cakes were boiled, Chaya spread them on a large, flat basket to cool. Later grated coconut and brown sugar would be provided, and the rice cakes would be dipped in the sugar and coconut as eaten.

Kondima crept down the ladder. There was Mookit in his back yard tending a row of bamboo lengths set up against a backing of

Jungle Thorn

live coals. The bamboos were about two and a half feet long. Each one had its mouth stuffed with a wad of banana leaf.

"Are you making that *pooloot* for the *Tuan*?" Kondima squatted down a little way from the fire.

"The *Tuan* likes *pooloot*," Mookit answered with dignity. He turned the long green sticks one by one. "My mother made enough cakes so everyone can have some.

"My mother made enough cakes for everybody, too," Kondima smiled.

"My mother learned to make this kind of cakes from the old teacher who was here before *Daud* came," Mookit spoke with considerable pride.

"Yes, I know, our people would never have known lots of things if the teachers hadn't come." Kondima spoke thoughtfully, "The *Tuan* will probably not get here until evening. I know he will be hungry."

The *pooloot* in the bamboo sticks boiled and bubbled. It smelled good. The sticky rice, called *pooloot*, was boiled in coconut milk. The green bamboo lengths were lined with a roll of banana leaf, young and tender. When the *pooloot* had swelled and filled the stick to the top, the charred bamboo was broken away and a long green roll came out. This was cut in slices like bologna.

"Oh, I just love *pooloot*!" Kondima said as she still squatted, watching Mookit at his work.

"If you love it so much, why don't you help me?" He looked hot and cross.

Kondima jumped up, and together the children moved the bamboos around until every one was well charred. Mookit set them up on the porch in the shade to cool.

"The *Tuan* is going to bring me a knife," Mookit smiled with much satisfaction. "D'you know why?"

Jungle Thorn

Kondima couldn't imagine any reason why the *Tuan* would want to bring Mookit anything at all. She said so.

"Well, missy," he said as he straddled the porch rail, "I carried all the water from the spring for him to wash his face the last time he was here. I carried all his tin cans away, too."

"Oh, yes, that wasn't so much," Kondima sniffed with scorn; "the tin cans had lids, didn't they? That's one of them right there in your kitchen. There's another hanging behind you."

Mookit wilted a little. "You wait and see, Kondima; the *Tuan* will bring my knife."

She turned toward her own doorway. It was always a contest to see who could get the tin cans the *Tuan* used for food and medicine. They were useful for cooking utensils. It seemed unfair that Mookit should actually be paid for carrying them home when everyone in the village wanted them.

Kondima played with Baby Bani for a while. Then as the sun began to sink over the western mountain, she slipped out of the house and stationed herself where she could watch the path leading down over the hill into the village.

"They come! They come!" shouted Mookit, who had established himself in a similar lookout station. "Look, the *Tuan* has two *bohongan*s." Mookit began to run up the hill. He couldn't take his eyes off the *bohongan*s. They are the large bark containers in which travelers in the jungle carry their belongings. Mookit's knife might be in one of them.

Kondima didn't run up the hill. She watched the gay company approach the native teacher's house. Then she crept home, hid herself under the mosquito net, and cried some hot, salty tears out of her one good eye.

Teacher **Daud's puppy does not look surprised at Kondima's sore eye.**

Chapter Two

Tuan Makes A Proposition

"I wish that His hands had been placed on my head,
That His arm had been thrown around me,
And that I might have seen His kind look when He said,
'Let the little ones come unto Me."

"CHILD, where are you?" Mother looked about in the gathering darkness. "Come, we are all going to the teacher's house to see the *Tuan*."

"Mother, I don't want to go," wailed the poor little girl.

"Hush, of course you must go." Mother drew her down the steep ladder.

Teacher *Daud's* house was full of eager, excited people greeting the *Tuan*. He was sitting on the floor talking to them, asking them about their children and their crops, and smiling at this one and that one. Kondima saw her own father shake hands with the *Tuan*.

"Are your children here?" asked *Tuan*.

"Yes, they are all here," Father smiled with pride. He handed Baby Bani to the *Tuan* so that he might lift the fine baby boy and see how heavy he was growing. Chaya stood behind her father shyly waiting. Presently he took her hand and drew her forward.

Jungle Thorn

"This is the big girl," said the *Tuan*, putting one arm around the child, "and where is the little lively one, Kondima?"

At this a number of people began calling, "Kondima, Kondima," in a loud voice. Mother thrust the embarrassed child forward; and then the *Tuan* saw.

A look of sharp pain crossed his sensitive face. He handed Baby Bani back to Father and released Chaya. As he cupped the little Kondima's chin in his hand and turned the sad little face up to his, there was nothing to be seen in the kind gray eyes but a warm smile of great friendliness. Then he drew the afflicted little one to his arms. He held her so all through the evening while he talked with the villagers and while they sang and prayed.

The baskets of cakes were passed around with the coconut and brown sugar. When the happy company broke up, everyone was sleepy. Mother had already taken Baby Bani home. Father took Kondima from *Tuan's* arms and started down the ladder.

"Wait a minute," the *Tuan* said as he laid a restraining hand on Father's arm, "wait just a minute. I want to talk with you." Father came back into the room and waited expectantly.

Chaya and Kondima sat on the ladder outside. "Your little Kondima has had a bad accident to her eye."

Then Father told him the whole sad story.

"It has been almost two moons already," Father sighed. "But what can we do? The eye is finished. No one can bring back the eye, even with the most powerful medicine."

"That is true." It was *Tuan's* deep, soft voice speaking again. "That is true, but we must save the other eye. If something is not done, she will lose the left eye, too, and be entirely blind." Then the missionary told Father that he would take Kondima down to his home at the big seaport town and find the best medicine possible to cure the fever and inflammation in the good eye. Father promised to think it over.

The unhappy parents talked about the *Tuan*'s proposition late into the night.

"I wonder if it would really do any good." Mother's voice held tears.

"She is so young," Father hesitated. "She has never been beyond our valley. Of course she would be homesick and cry all the time. She would make the *Tuan*'s family very miserable with her crying." There was silence for a moment.

"I am afraid of the white man's medicine. Is it not commonly reported that the white people steal the jungle children and use their hearts and their livers to make medicine? I have heard that they shoot people with a gun like a thorn. People go to sleep for hours after being shot with such a gun, and they are even cut open. That's when they take their hearts and livers out for medicine."

"I don't believe those stories." Father turned restlessly. "I don't think they steal people."

Mother was silent for a long time; then she spoke with firm decision. "No! I will not let her go, I might never see my child again. What has happened, has happened. We will let it be as it is." Then Father began to argue that it might be a good thing to try the white man's medicine.

"The *Tuan* is very kind," he began. "He has little ones of his own. He would let no harm come to her. Did you not see how kindly he held her tonight?

But Mother had made up her mind.

Kondima, listening from her mat in the corner, turned her face to the wall and cried herself to sleep.

"Kondima, oh, Kondima," Mookit's voice rose in a gay shout. Kondima opened the door just a little.

Jungle Thorn

Mookit and Alijah were standing at the foot of the ladder.

"My knife, my knife! " cried Mookit, waving a bright object round his head. "You said *Tuan* wouldn't bring it, but he did, he did! "

Kondima slammed the door as hard as she could, seeing it was open such a little way, but nothing could shut out Mookit's and Alijah's laughter. Kondima went to the far side of the hut and looked out the only window. *Tuan* and Teacher *Daud* were standing over by the teacher's house. Snatches of their conversation reached the little girl's keen ears.

"We must have a school for them, *Daud*; the boys should learn to work with wood and iron. The girls should learn to sew and cook and care for children. All of them should learn to read and write." Teacher *Daud* nodded, and there was more talk which Kondima couldn't hear. Then they both turned and walked up the ladder into *Daud's* house.

Teacher *Daud* had been in the village for six months already, and Kondima knew that it had been planned from the time he came that a school should be established. But there were many fears from many things to be overcome in the hearts of the villagers; they could not see the advantage of sending their girls to school to learn reading and writing when they would never do anything but tend babies, cook rice, and care for the gardens and pigs. There might be some reason for boys to go to school, but the villagers were doubtful even in regard to this, so the school which the native teacher had often talked about had not yet been started.

"I think I'll go over and play with Teacher *Daud's* puppy." Kondima opened the door and started down the ladder. Angry as she was, it was still disappointing to see no one about. Actually she wanted very much to see Mookit's knife. The puppy was only an excuse.

The little girl walked straight to the teacher's house. The puppy was playing on the grass in the shade of a coconut tree. She threw herself down beside him, laid her face against his long silky ear, and cried,

Tuan Makes A Proposition

"Dear puppy, I wish I could be a puppy, too. Nobody likes to see me any more. Mookit and Alijah are so mean, and I can't go to the *Tuan*'s house." The puppy turned and licked her face with grave sympathy.

"Kondima."

She turned at the sound of a pleasant voice and looked up to see *Tuan* standing in the door of Teacher *Daud's* house.

"Did you help make the cakes we had last night?"

Kondima's heart warmed with pleasure.

Tuan came down the ladder and sat down on the grass beside the puppy. He drew Kondima close, and they sat quietly for some time. She looked up at the side of Teacher *Daud's* house. There were six baskets nailed to the wall. *Daud's* hens slept in those fine bedchambers every night. *Daud* called each hen by name. They were good, well-trained hens. Every night after they had supper of unhusked rice and table scraps, *Daud* would call each one to him. He would lift her and set her feet in a pan of clean water and wash all the dust from her feet. With a clean cloth he would wash and polish the beak of each chickabiddy and then thrust her into the little door of her bedroom basket.

Jungle Thorn

"All those hens lack is a good-night kiss," laughed *Tuan* the first time he saw *Daud* put them to bed. The puppy, too, was clean and fat. *Daud* bought canned milk for the puppy whenever he went down to the big city forty miles away. He never bought any milk for himself, but he always carried a few cans in his *bohongan*s; so the puppy might have a special treat. The puppy had a bath in warm soapy water every day, too. Teacher *Daud* explained that since he had no wife and no children, the only way he could set a good example was to take good care of his pets.

Kondima looked at the baskets; then she looked at the puppy. "The *Tuan* and *Daud* are both just good, that's what they are."

Tuan pulled the puppy into his lap. "I want to tell you a story, Kondima."

The little girl waited expectantly.

"Once there was a little girl about as big as you are right now. She was a pretty little girl, and she went about singing merry songs all day long, making everyone happy with her cheerful ways. Then one day a sad thing happened. This little girl was walking along the road with her sister when a naughty girl picked up a stone and threw it. It just happened that this pretty little girl turned her head at the very moment the stone was thrown, and it hit her right in the face. Oh, how that stone hurt the poor little girl! It broke her nice, straight little nose and made her sick for a long time. She never was very strong after that.

"The little girl could never be proud any more, for her face was no longer pretty. She was sick and miserable most of the time."

Kondima searched *Tuan*'s face with such eagerness that the gray eyes grew misty for just an instant. "*Tuan*, did anyone ever like the little girl any more?"

"Oh, yes, that is the wonderful part of the story. You see, the little girl was very lonely at first, and so she learned to talk with Jesus. When she couldn't sleep at night, she would talk to Him and be comforted.

Tuan Makes A Proposition

She became so sweet and gentle in all her ways that she was loved more than most people are, in spite of her disfigured face. She lived a long and happy life."

"What was the little girl's name, *Tuan*?" questioned Kondima.

"Her name was Ellen," *Tuan* smiled down at her.

The warm feeling began to come back to Kondima's heart, her throat cleared, and she took a deep breath. The little brown hand found its way into the big, strong one, and they sat for a long time looking out across the purple valley. *Daud* found them thus when he came back from the spring with the rice all washed and ready to put over the fire.

Kondima jumped up with a little of her old-time energy. She had forgotten about Mookit, but there was Mookit sitting on the ladder to her own house. He thrust a rudely carved doll into her hands. "See, Kondima, I made this baby for you the first thing; aren't you glad the *Tuan* gave me the knife?"

The toy was a simple one, but in Kondima's eyes it was wonderful. She hugged the crude baby to her breast in ecstasy. "Oh, Mookit, how did you do it?"

Thus forgiven and reinstated, Mookit became eloquent. "It is a magic knife." He took it from his pocket. "I will make you a little rice huller and a buffalo cart like they have down in the city." Then he drew out a small stick of soft wood. After handing the knife to Kondima so she could feel its sharpness, he showed her how easily the wood was cut.

"See, it has three blades." He opened them all out fanwise. "No one in this village has so good a knife; I will keep it as long as I live."

When Kondima woke the following morning, the *Tuan* had gone. Teacher *Daud* was singing in his house. The village had returned to its usual quiet round of daily duties.

"Tell Kokit's daughter to come over here," *Daud* called to Kondima. It was only a step from Kondima's house to the hut of Kokit's daughter,

Jungle Thorn

who strapped her small baby to her back and followed Kondima.

On the floor in the teacher's house was a pile of clothing. There were several small garments. *Daud* began pulling these out.

"Are you going to give these to me for my baby?" The eyes of Kokit's daughter widened with surprise.

"Yes, *Tuan* told me that you must have some warm things for the baby so he won't get sick like your other ones did."

"The *Tuan* is very good," said Kokit's daughter as she rolled the garments into a neat bundle.

"You may have this little blanket, too." *Daud* handed over a pink checked blanket bound with wide binding.

"Your baby will be like the son of a rajah now," laughed the young teacher. "Here is a little pot of rubbing medicine for your father. Tell him to warm it over the fire before putting it on his body."

During the day Kondima heard other people called to *Daud's* house. All of them went away with some token of the *Tuan's* kind thoughtfulness, but for Kondima herself *Tuan* had left nothing. Oh, yes, he had left something. Kondima tried to think what it was that *Tuan* had left. It was the story, the story about the little girl who was hit in the face by the stone. After all, Kondima's family were not poor. They did not need clothing. It was the poor of the village that had been remembered.

That night after Kondima went to bed, she thought for a long time about the little girl whose face had been spoiled by a cruel stone. As she lay quietly under her mosquito curtain, she asked of the soft darkness, "Jesus, are You here? Will You be a friend to me like You were to the little girl *Tuan* told me about?"

For the first time since the accident Kondima fell asleep without crying.

Chapter Three

King of the Centipedes

"But thousands and thousands who stumble and fall
Never heard of that wonderful home;
I should like them to know there is room for them all
And that Jesus has bid them to come."

No. THEY won't let her go." Alijah drew herself up to her full height. She was the center of attraction for the moment, and she meant to make the most of it. "Kondima, you tell them what the *Tuan* said. Tell them why your father won't let you go to the *Tuan's* house."

Kondima hung her head and said nothing. She had come to the spring to wash the rice for dinner. She squatted down where the stream of clear water trickled from the bamboo trough into the pool, and began washing the rice.

Kokit's daughter lifted her full bamboo. "No wonder," she sniffed; "who knows what medicine those white people would use on a small child?" The group of women there seemed to disagree in their opinion. Even as the village was part heathen and part Christian, so the talk of the women followed a divided pattern.

"If the *Tuan* offered to take my child to his house, I would be very glad," Mookit's mother said as she let down her long dark hair and began washing it with a bar of red soap. "As for the medicine, I

27

think our own medicine men have much to learn from the white men. Does not your own father use the *Tuan's* rubbing medicine?"

The daughter of Kokit set her heavy water bamboos down again. "Look here, my friend, have you never heard how the white people steal the brown children of the forest, and they are never heard of again? It is a well-known fact that they use their hearts and livers for medicine." After saying this the heathen woman gathered up her bamboos and departed from the spring in scornful dignity.

"Do not be angry with her," said the mother of Mookit; "the poor thing has had trouble enough. Fancy having borne three boys and losing them all. No wonder she is sour. I hope this little one lives." She waved her hand toward the retreating figure of Kokit's daughter with a small brown baby tied to her back.

It was true as the women at the spring had said. Kokit's daughter had lost her three older children—all boys. Her heart had been well-nigh broken by these sad bereavements, as everyone in the village knew, and she would not allow the new baby out of her sight lest some harm come

Kokit's daughter held her sick baby in her arms for a long, long time.

Jungle Thorn

to him. He was a fine boy, just old enough to reach for bright objects with his fat little hands.

"Older sister"—it was Kondima's voice at the door—"may I come in and play with the baby?"

"Oh, do come in," called the voice of the young mother. She laid the baby down at once on a mat. Kondima unstrapped Baby Bani from her own shoulders, then spent a gay half hour with the two tiny folk. Kondima found much satisfaction in playing with the babies. They were too young to notice her eye. They loved a soft voice and a gentle touch, and they laughed and gurgled as generously as babies do anywhere in the wide world.

"Today we go to the *baboolian*." (The *baboolian* was a witch doctor.) Kokit's daughter began laying out a change of clothing, also some of the baby's new garments received the day before from Teacher *Daud*.

"No one is sick," said Kondima; "why do you go to the *baboolian*?"

"It is this way," Kokit's daughter said and smiled. "You see our baby is a fine healthy fellow. I am very anxious that no harm shall come to him. His father is going to give a water buffalo to the *baboolian* so that he may make powerful charms that will protect our baby from all evil things."

"That is nice!" Kondima patted one of the baby's fat legs. "When will you return?"

"We will return tomorrow, and will you please ask Chaya to feed our pigs tomorrow morning?" The young woman bustled about making preparations to depart.

"Older sister," Kondima hesitated, "why is it bad for me to go to the *Tuan's* house? I want to go very much."

Kokit's daughter paused a moment in her preparations. "Why

30

King of the Centipedes

don't you come with me to the *baboolian*? He would make medicine for you."

"Could he cure my eye, do you think?" the little girl questioned with eager interest.

"Well," the young woman evaded, "it would be a difficult thing to do. Perhaps he could if your father was willing to give him a couple of water buffalo and his best brass gong. Really I don't know, Kondima. The *baboolian* has taught me to fear the white man's medicine very much."

"Father," began Kondima when her father was seated before his evening plate of rice, "do you think that the *baboolian* could make medicine for me?"

Father lifted his eyes with an apprehensive scowl. "Who has been talking to you about the witch doctor?" he demanded.

Kondima hung her head. "Kokit's daughter is taking the baby over there to have the *baboolian* make charms and medicine so he won't get sick and die like the rest of her children. I just wondered if he could help my eye. "

"Kokit's daughter runs too much to the *baboolian*." Father began eating again. "It is true he makes powerful medicine; but since we began to follow the Jesus teaching, I much distrust the charms and witchcraft. I would not allow the *baboolian* to make medicine for any of my family."

Next morning Mother prepared a plate of warm food for blind Kokit. She knew he would be alone all day. The food was sent over by the hand of Chaya, who was also delegated to feed the pigs.

"Why is it I hate pigs so much?" Chaya made a wry face as she climbed the ladder into the hut. "I just guess pigs are the dirtiest animals in all the world. If it wasn't for pigs, our village would be nice and clean."

Jungle Thorn

It was true. The pigs were a genuine curse to Durian village. None of the Christian people kept pigs, but all the heathen did. The filthy razor-back animals had the run of the place. Chaya and Kondima had received a little packet of flower seed from *Tuan*. They had planted with ambitious hope, even building a little fence about the plants, but all to no avail. The pigs had broken through and rooted up every little green shoot. From that day forward both girls hated pigs with a deep and bitter hatred. It was a real cross for Chaya to feed them even though Mother reminded her that it was a necessary courtesy.

"The daughter of Kokit has returned." Chaya looked out the one window of the hut into the late afternoon sunshine. "I will run over and see what charms she has brought." She hurried down the ladder. At first Kondima started to follow, then she turned back sadly.

Mother noticed the child's hesitation. "Why don't you go, too?" she asked, and her eyes looked warm and kind.

"No, Mother, many people will come in to talk, and they will all look at my eye. I will not go."

In about an hour Chaya returned breathless with excitement. "Oh, Mother, Daddy, may I go tomorrow to hunt centipedes?"

The parents looked at each other in surprise.

"Why do you want to hunt centipedes?" Mother questioned.

"The *baboolian* gave Kokit's daughter three powerful charms for the baby," Chaya began, "but none of them will be any good unless they can find a centipede with rainbow colors on its back, and it must be as big as this." She measured a full twelve inches on her slender brown arm.

"Did they give the *baboolian* the water buffalo?" Father inquired.

"Oh, Father, of course they did. How would he be willing to make all the charms unless he was satisfied with the water buffalo?"

32

King of the Centipedes

"But, child"—Father stood up and looked down at his small daughter—"what is the use of the centipede? What will they do with it?"

Chaya returned her father's gaze with steady courage. "That is a secret, Father, they will tell no one; but Kokit's daughter told me that her husband will give a roll of fine black cloth to whoever finds the best centipede."

"I suppose all the village children will hunt centipedes tomorrow. Very likely no one in the village will do anything else." Mother looked disgusted. "You may go tomorrow, but one day is enough to spend at such business."

"May Kondima go, too?" Chaya looked at her little sister.

"Yes, in fact I shan't let you go without her." Father spoke with firmness, but he smiled at Kondima as he picked up Baby Bani and tossed him in the air.

On the following day, as Mother had predicted, every child in the village hunted centipedes. Every old log in the clearing was turned over. Some of the braver of the children even entered the edge of the jungle to tear the bark from the old trees. Some of the men joined in the hunt, for the reward offered was attractive.

The day closed with many centipedes found. They were of all

sizes and shades of color. Gooloon, the husband of Kokit's daughter, carried the whole collection to the *baboolian*. Mookit begged to go with him and was allowed to carry the basket of centipedes. Kondima and Chaya watched them until they were out of sight.

"How I wish I was a boy!" said Kondima. "I would love to hear what the *baboolian* will say when he sees a whole basket of centipedes."

It was some hours before the travelers returned. Mookit was swinging the empty basket, and Gooloon looked tired.

"Tell us, what did the *baboolian* say?" The children were upon Mookit before he could get to his own doorway. In fact, he was in no great hurry to get anywhere; he had a story and was eager to tell it.

"The *baboolian* said that none of the centipedes we brought were any good. He just waved his hand like this"—he made a broad

King of the Centipedes

sweep of both brown hands—"and he said, 'Take these miserable things away! Not one of them is suitable! The king of the centipedes must be found; no other will do!'"

"What did you do with the centipedes?" Alijah took the empty basket from her cousin's hand.

"I just emptied them under the *baboolian*'s house. They were of no value."

"Oh, Mookit! "Kondima clapped both hands. "Then we will have to hunt again. Maybe I will find the king of the centipedes."

The next day fewer people joined in the hunt. On the third day only three continued. Gooloon raised the reward to two rolls of black cloth and a brass gong. This stimulated the fading interest of the people, and a larger crowd joined the search on the fourth day.

By this time the whole area near the village had been well searched. Mookit's family were going to their rice field that day. It was in a small clearing about a mile from Durian village. Kondima begged to go along and was allowed to accompany the family. This was not at all unusual. Often several of the village children would go along on such excursions to the new rice field. There were many things small folk could do. On this particular day the small folk had no intention of doing anything but hunt. They were going to hunt for the king of the centipedes. Now these were Christian people, but they saw no harm in looking for the centipede even though the heathen witch doctor wanted it for a charm.

Mookit and Kondima turned over all the small logs in the clearing. "Father, help us turn this big log." The small boy tugged at a thick slab of black, wetlooking wood. Whosh! Over the log went with a plop! And there under it was the largest centipede any of them had ever seen.

"Look, look, Father, the king of the centipedes!

Jungle Thorn

Mookit darted after the creature which was slithering away under another log. He headed it off, and Father plumped a piece of bark down over it until he could devise some way of capturing it alive and without injury. The *baboolian* had said the centipede must be perfect.

When the planters returned to the village that afternoon, Mookit carried a tight bark bundle. He headed straight for the house of Kokit.

"Oh, Mookit, what have you got in the package?" Alijah hurried up to him. Several other children joined her. Mookit spoke not a word to any of them, but he called, "Gooloon, Gooloon, come out."

Gooloon's shaggy head appeared in the door.

"I have brought the king of the centipedes," Mookit announced with pride. The excitement of the gathering crowd of villagers mounted by the second. Gooloon descended the ladder and took the bark container from Mookit's hand. He drew a deep, tight basket from the wall of the hut and proceeded to open the parcel over the big basket. The evening sunshine fell on an enormous centipede nearly fifteen inches long. Its dark body shone with iridescent colors in the evening light. A cry of admiration and wonder burst from every beholder.

"What a centipede! Verily the king of them all!

Gooloon rubbed his hands together with satisfaction.

"We will carry it to the *baboolian* tomorrow, Mookit," Gooloon assured the small boy. "If he approves it, you shall have your two rolls of black cloth and the brass gong."

Mookit retired to his own house covered with glory.

Through Kondima's dreams marched the king of the centipedes. He was bigger than a water buffalo and she counted his legs over and over again, but there were always more than she could count.

Gooloon and Mookit hurried to the *baboolian* the next day and returned late in the afternoon. They went at once to Gooloon's hut; and when Mookit came out, he was carrying the reward. Gooloon's face was wreathed in smiles.

"The *baboolian* was very pleased," Mookit said as he sat with Kondima on the ladder of his own hut. "His eyes glittered, and he rubbed his hands together like this." Mookit bent over and bared his teeth and mimicked the *baboolian*. "He told Gooloon to grind the centipede between two stones until it is a soft paste. Then he must make a warm broth of it and feed it all to the baby. The *baboolian* says no harm can ever come to the baby after he has eaten such powerful medicine."

"I think Gooloon is grinding the centipede now," said Kondima, shuddering as she heard the noise of two heavy stones at the rear of Kokit's hut.

Teacher *Daud* had been visiting in a neighboring village for a few days. Kondima saw him return just as the sun went down. She wanted to tell him about the centipede, but it was already dark when she and Mookit had finished talking. There was no light in *Daud's* hut.

"He must have been very tired and have gone to bed already," thought the little girl. "I will get up early in the morning and be the first to tell him."

So it turned out that Kondima was sitting on her ladder when Teacher *Daud* passed on his way to the spring the next morning. His towel and soap and toothbrush were all rolled up together under his arm. He called a cheerful "Good morning" as he passed. Kondima started to run after him.

At that moment the voice of loud wailing broke out in Kokit's hut. *Daud* dropped his towel and toothbrush and sprang through the door.

Jungle Thorn

"Adoh! Adoh! my child, my child!" It was the voice of Kokit's daughter.

Kondima crept up the ladder and peeked in. The daughter of Kokit sat on the floor with her baby dead in her arms. Her long hair hung in wild confusion around her pale and terror-stricken face. Kondima joined her small voice in loud wails, and within a few minutes the whole village had assembled. The lamentations that grew louder every moment would have melted the heart of the *baboolian* himself.

Little by little Teacher *Daud* drew the story from Gooloon. The broth of the centipede had been fed to the baby the night before, and he had gone to sleep at once. It was not until morning that they had found the baby dead under his little blanket. *Daud's* tears mingled with those of the parents. He reproached himself for having been away.

"I could have prevented this," he said over and over again.

With tender sympathy the Christian villagers comforted the sad parents. *Daud* buried the baby with a few words of exhortation to the villagers.

"My poor suffering friends," he addressed Gooloon and his wife as he sat with them the following evening, "come with us and follow Jesus. He loved the little children. He will give back your little ones. Forsake the hard way of the *baboolian* and find peace to your hearts."

All the neighbors bowed their heads and wept anew. So it came about that from that day the daughter of Kokit and Gooloon, her husband, began to listen to the Christian teaching.

Since their huts were close together, the daughter of Kokit came often to Kondima's house. She found much comfort in playing with Baby Bani. Little by little she revived from her deep sorrow and talked much with mother about the Jesus teaching.

Chapter Four

The Answer Is Yes

"I long for that glorious and beautiful time,
The fairest, the dearest, and best,
When the dear little children of every clime
Shall crowd to His arms and be blest."

THE *TUAN* comes! The *Tuan* comes!" Alijah's shrill little voice was heard far up the mountainside. Kondima and Chaya were winnowing rice where they had spread a big mat in the shade of the durian tree. Both girls looked up.

"Is it really the *Tuan*, Chaya?" Kondima strained her left eye, but it was now so inflamed and sore that it was hard to see very far.

"There are two *tuan*s," Chaya said as she shaded her eyes with her hand. "One of them is our *Tuan*; the other one I never saw before. He is taller. Mookit and Alijah are running to meet them."

Chaya dropped her winnowing basket and walked around the house to get a better view of the party.

"Kondima, is that really the *Tuan*?" Mother called from the hut. "It has only been one moon since he was here. I wonder why he returns so quickly."

"It is really the *Tuan*, Mother." The little girl climbed the ladder into the house and took up her station at the window where she could watch everything without being seen.

The Tuan and his brother, the Guru, visited the village where Kondima lived.

The Answer Is Yes

There were two *tuan*s. Kondima could see them very well now. They had stopped in the shade of the coconut tree by the house of Teacher *Daud*. There were two carriers. One of them Kondima knew as Sibaniel, the *Tuan's* gardener; the other was a stranger. The new *tuan* was tall and not so thin as "our *Tuan*. "The villagers gave him a name at once-the Guru-since they were told that he was the teacher from the great school in Singapore. Both the men appeared tired. *Daud* had just sent Mookit up the coconut tree to knock down some green nuts. The *bohongan*s were placed against the wall of *Daud's* house, and the whole company was watching Mookit scramble up the tree like a monkey. In a few minutes he had kicked off several large green coconuts. He hung onto the stems and fronds at the top of the tree and used his right foot to push off the heavy nuts.

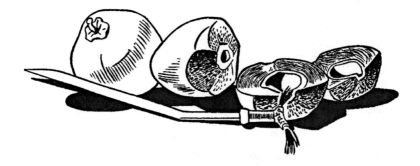

"That's enough," the *Tuan* shouted to the small boy. "We shall want some coconuts another day." Mookit kicked off three more and then slid down the sloping trunk of the tree. *Daud* fetched his big chopping knife from the hut. With a heavy stroke he cut off the top of each nut neatly with one blow. This left a little hole about an inch across. The nuts were passed around to the visitors, who seated themselves on the grass and began to drink refreshing draughts of the delicious coconut milk.

When the nuts were empty, they were handed back to *Daud*, who

Jungle Thorn

split them wide open with his knife and fashioned a little shovel of the tough shell for each person. Then they all scooped out the soft meat of the green coconut and ate it with evident relish.

By this time all the villagers knew that two white men had come. People were coming from all directions. Everyone was full of curiosity about the visitor. Kondima longed to join her parents and Chaya as they followed the eager crowd to Teacher *Daud's* house, but something held her back. She could see and hear everything from her station at the window.

"This is my brother," said the *Tuan*, laughing. "Doesn't he look like me?" Someone ventured to say that he didn't think they looked at all alike. "Well, his wife and my wife are sisters; doesn't that make us brothers?" Everyone thought that was a good joke.

"You should have sent word that you were coming," said Mookit's mother. "We would have prepared cakes and curry and given you a fine welcome."

"Come, I will help you prepare the meal for the *Tuan*." It was Kokit's daughter speaking. The two women came down the hill to Kokit's house. Kondima joined them there and lent her best effort to grating the coconut and washing the vegetables.

Kokit's daughter ran to the spring with the rice kettle while Mookit's mother kindled the fire on the flat earthen stove. It was only a short time until the rice was boiling. An hour later a satisfying meal was set before the visitors.

It was dark now. Kondima ventured into the shadows near the door of *Daud's* house. There was only one feeble kerosene lamp burning in the house. Finally, drawn by the urge to see and hear all that was going on, she crept up the ladder and into the house, crouching down behind blind Kokit, who had been led in by his son-in-law, Gooloon.

Mookit, who was usually very much in evidence on any social

occasion, was nowhere to be seen. He had grieved deeply over his part in finding the king of the centipedes that had caused the death of Gooloon's baby. Teacher *Daud* had tried to comfort the small boy.

"I can't forget how Kokit's daughter cried that morning," Mookit would say with sorrow.

Kondima saw Gooloon and his wife sitting close to the *Tuan* and guessed the reason for Mookit's absence.

"And where is Kondima?" *Tuan* had been talking with Teacher *Daud*. "Will someone bring Kondima? I want to see her." The unhappy little girl was dragged from her place of concealment and pushed toward the *Tuan*. With a bright smile he received her and drew her down onto his knee, then continued his conversation with Teacher *Daud*: "I hope this child's parents have changed their minds about my proposition." *Tuan* looked down at Kondima.

"Her eye is no better. Have you discussed the matter with them?"

Teacher *Daud* spoke in a low voice, "They are very sorry they refused your invitation. They can see that the eye is getting worse every day. I think they will be willing this time; wait and see."

"Would you like to go to my house, little one?" he whispered into the little brown ear. "There are seven children there," he confided, "two little boys and two little girls, a big boy and two big girls. Yes, there is a baby, too; that makes eight all together. The little ones are Nancy, Peter, June, and Bennie. They will play with you. They are all expecting you."

Kondima wriggled happily; she looked out from under her thatch of tangled black hair at Father. He was smiling, so she knew the answer was Yes. Thereupon she swung off into a dream of such magnificence as can scarcely be imagined.

The conversation went on and on. Teacher *Daud* was relating the sad story of Gooloon's baby and the *baboolian*. Mookit, who had been

Jungle Thorn

hiding, crept around where he could look at the *Tuan's* face. As the story progressed to its mournful climax, he could find nothing in those kind gray eyes but deep sympathy.

Mercifully Teacher *Daud* omitted the name of the person who had been successful in the quest for the king of the centipedes, and *Tuan* did not inquire.

"My friends, do not grieve more." The deep, kind voice was husky with emotion. The *Tuan* looked first at Gooloon, then at his weeping wife. "See, we are all your friends. Very likely God will give you more little ones, and you will trust them to His mercies rather than to the charms of the *baboolian*. That will be a much better way."

Both the men then commended the Father for his change of heart in allowing Kondima to accompany the *Tuan* down to the great city. Very gently they broke the news to him that it would be necessary to send Kondima to Singapore, a great city days away by steamship. This was a terrible trial for the poor man. "How can I let her go so far away among strangers?

"Will she not die of homesickness? It will be as though she was dead and buried out on the mountainside with Gooloon's baby." Father held his head in his hands for a long time. Finally he raised troubled eyes to search the *Tuan's* face with desperate eagerness. "Will you take her there yourself?" he questioned.

"No," answered the kindly man, "but here is my brother who has two little daughters of his own. He is returning to Singapore in four days, and he has promised to care for the child as his own."

Father turned his gaze on the Guru and studied his face for a full minute. The kind blue eyes looking straight into his own held nothing but great friendliness and understanding.

"Will you go with these men, Kondima?" Her father spoke in a stern and husky voice.

The Answer Is Yes

For answer the little girl threw both arms around the *Tuan's* neck and hid her face on his shoulder.

Father held out his hand to the Guru. "She may go," he said and arose at once. Taking Kondima in his arms, he picked his way through the darkness to his own hut.

Again Kondima lay awake on her mat straining her ears to hear what Father and Mother were saying.

"I have told the *Tuan* that she may go." Father's voice sounded weary and confused.

"I suppose it is best," Mother agreed after a long silence. "She grows worse every day. What good will she ever be blind—blind and useless? What man will ever want her for a wife? It is hard to look at her. I can hardly bear to look at her myself."

Early next morning Kondima hurried to the spring. Yes, she was really hard to look at. She gazed into the clear pool with a shudder. The ruined eye was a horrible gray mass protruding from the eye socket so the lid could not be closed. The other eye was red and sore. The black hair was tangled. The face was miserable and sad. Yes, she was most repulsive to look at. Yet *Tuan* had looked at her with the greatest tenderness, and he had held her in his arms all evening. That was why she wanted to go with *Tuan*. He loved her in spite of her disfigured face, and she loved him back with all her strength made doubly strong through suffering.

"I am going with the *Tuan*." Kondima came upon Mookit just going down to the spring to fetch water for his mother. "I will go tomorrow. It is very possible I shall stay a long time if I like it. I may even become one of his children."

Mookit looked defeated. He mumbled something about wishing he had a sore eye so he could go down to the *Tuan's* house. Kondima scarcely heard him.

"Alijah, I am going to the *Tuan's* house." Mookit's little cousin had come around the corner of the hut. Kondima could not keep from telling the good news to everyone. "I will see his house and all his children." She swept her hand across the valley with a gesture that signified a great multitude of children. "It will be very useful for me to see all those things," she meditated. "I shall probably stay with the *Tuan* after this."

"Chaya, do you think I might get to ride on one of those 'going' things like buffalo carts without any animal to pull them? I have heard Father say there are many of them in the city." Again she would ask, "Chaya, do you know there is a great valley of water beyond our mountain? It is like a great plain. I have heard Father tell about it."

Kondima did not mention her need of medical attention as one of her reasons for going with the *Tuan*. Indeed it did not seem so important now. Yet her eye was rapidly growing worse. She sometimes wondered how many more days she would be able to look upon the green mountain and the loved faces of her family and friends.

The Answer Is Yes

That evening the whole village gathered at Teacher *Daud's* house to sing. The night was filled with sweet melody as the soft voices rang out in the clear mountain air.

"I would rather hear these people sing than to hear the angels," smiled *Tuan* at *Daud*.

"Why, *Tuan*?" *Daud* replied in surprise. "It should be a great privilege to hear angels sing."

Tuan nodded. "It would be, of course, but no angel can ever know the darkness and suffering out of which these songs have grown in the hearts of these people. That makes them sweeter to me than any other music."

When the villagers scattered to their homes, they kept on singing; and up from a score of tiny brown huts were wafted the sweet tones of the evening hymn. Tears came to Kondima's eye. She was leaving tomorrow. Would she ever hear the songs of the village again? She crept into her mosquito curtain and talked softly in the darkness with that great Friend of little children. Then hugging her wooden dolly close, she drifted into dreamless sleep.

Kondima takes the Tuan's **hand and goes through the forest to the road**

Chapter Five

Beyond The Blue Mountain

"But still to the Saviour in prayer we may go,
And ask for a share in His love,
And if we thus earnestly seek Him below,
We shall see Him and hear Him above."

CHAYA! "It was Kondima's voice calling in the early dawn. "Chaya, wake up! This is the day 1 am going with the *Tuan*." Chaya turned on her mat and opened sleepy eyes. "Look, Chaya." Kondima exhibited a large piece of palm bark the color and thickness of heavy brown paper. It was the sheath of the *penang* palm leaf. "Look, Chaya, I am going to wrap my baby in this." She picked up the rude dolly Mookit had carved for her. "I am going to wrap my baby in this so no harm will come while I am gone."

By this time Chaya was fully awake. She sat I up, parted the mosquito net, and looked about in the small, dark hut. Her eyes rested on the beam which crossed the length of the hut overhead. It was held in place by heavy thongs of rattan. "Why not tie the bundle to that beam with a string of bark? I can climb up there and fasten it." Kondima approved this idea, and Chaya scrambled up over the window and out onto the naked beams of the little house. With deft fingers she tied the precious bundle to the beam.

Jungle Thorn

Having thus disposed of her one prized possession, Kondima was ready to depart. She looked out the small window. *Tuan* and Sibaniel were already outside *Daud's* house with one of the *bohongans*. The Guru was just putting the cover on his *bohongan*. Kondima could see him through the door of *Daud's* house.

Father was talking with *Tuan* in a low voice. Kondima could not catch the words of the conversation. Mother came in the door. She had just returned from the spring. Her eyes were red with crying, but when she looked at Kondima, she smiled. "Come, child," she urged, "the *Tuan* is ready to go; you must not delay him. Be a good girl and do exactly as he says. May God's blessing go with you." Taking Kondima by the hand, she led her to the *Tuan*.

Father walked with the party to the top of the hill. Then with a few short words of farewell he turned back. Mookit was not yet awake; neither was Alijah. None of the village children had wakened. It was still very early. So with scarcely a ripple on the surface of its busy life, Kondima passed out of the village. She did not even turn back to look down over the cluster of brown huts on the mountainside. *Tuan* did not stop or look back. He walked into the jungle and the steep narrow path that led away beyond the blue mountain.

Kondima looked down at her dress. It was old, ragged, and much faded. It didn't seem to have any special color any more. It was Chaya who had the new dresses now, and Kondima wore the old ones. "I don't care," she insisted to herself; "if my clothes are not nice to look at, people will take less notice of me. After all, what is the use of pretty clothes for a little girl nobody wants to look at?"

Having nothing to carry but his camera, which was slung over his shoulder by a strap, *Tuan* had both his hands free. Kondima took possession of one.

"Are you a good traveler, little one?" *Tuan* looked down at his

Beyond The Blue Mountain

small companion. "We have a long journey before us today." Kondima smiled, but said nothing. Her bare brown feet kept time with the swing of the *bohongan*s on the backs of the carriers. The only sound was the creak of the heavy thongs as the big bark containers swayed back and forth.

The tall forest trees arched overhead. The wellbeaten path was damp and slippery. On both sides great ferns and thick brush made a green wall. Down below the ridge a family of monkeys chattered and called to one another in the morning stillness.

"Look, look, *Tuan*! "Kondima pointed to a dark object on the bare leg of Sibaniel, who was trudging along just ahead of them.

"Sibaniel, stop! You have a leech," called *Tuan*.

Sibaniel set down the *bohongan* and screwed his neck around to see the back of his leg. With a broad grin he came back to where *Tuan* was already on his knees opening a small packet of first-aid materials he always carried in his pocket. Drawing out a small vial of iodine, he directed a single drop to the point where the leech had fastened into the flesh. Under five pairs of watchful eyes the surprised leech withdrew his spearhead attack and dropped off onto the path. Sibaniel picked up a sharp stone and ended the leech's career at once in a manner which met with Kondima's hearty approval.

"Why can't you just pull the leech off?" questioned the Guru.

"The wound would bleed terribly, and you might pull off the body of the leech and leave his head embedded in the flesh. This would make a nasty infected sore," said *Tuan* as they hurried on their way.

"If enough leeches fastened onto a person, they could suck enough blood out to cause great weakness or even death."

After this all of them were wary of leeches. More than twenty times they saw the small creatures drop from the wet branches, expecting to settle on warm brown flesh; but each of the travelers was

Jungle Thorn

on the look-out, and not another leech was able to make a successful attack on the company.

As they walked along the path, the two white men engaged in conversation, but Kondima could not understand what they said. Sibaniel spoke in the Dusun language and called her attention to various things as they climbed up and down the steep trail.

"When we get down in the valley beyond the next hill," he said in a merry voice, "I will find you a ripe durian. Maybe I will find two or three of them." They jogged along another half mile.

"Do you see the blue mountain yonder?" Sibaniel indicated a high ridge far ahead. "When we reach the very top, you will be able to see the ocean." A look of pain and embarrassment clouded his jolly face as the child answered.

"Perhaps I shall not be able to see so far, Sibaniel."

The party descended into the valley along an open hillside where someone had cleared the forest and raised a crop of rice the previous season. The sun shone down with intense heat although it was not yet nine o'clock in the morning,

"Look and see if these farmers have left any cucumbers by chance." *Tuan* stopped and wiped the perspiration from his forehead. Sibaniel set down the *bohongan* and scouted around the edge of the clearing. He came back in a few minutes with two large cucumbers. They were almost ripe, but they were full of juice and cool because they had been lying deep in the shade of tangled vines and brush. The field was abandoned after harvest, so any passer-by was welcome to any vegetables remaining in the field.

"Come, come," *Tuan* smiled, "this will make a nice, clean drink for us." He handed his sharp pocket knife to Sibaniel, who peeled both cucumbers and divided them among all five travelers. After this refreshing interlude the little company proceeded with renewed energy

Beyond The Blue Mountain

and were soon in the valley of the durian trees. Coming to a glade in the forest, they all sat down to rest for a few minutes. The two carriers did not recline long on the green grass. They disappeared into the jungle by a scarcely discernible path, and shortly afterward their shouts could be heard from far below.

"They have found durians." Kondima smiled with satisfaction. Even the *Tuan* looked cheerful. In a few minutes the two Dusuns emerged from the forest with durians dangling from both hands.

"I declare, I wonder how anything can smell so awful and taste so good! "It was the Guru who spoke. Sibaniel was sharpening a blunt stick which he bored into the end of a durian. The fruit was as large as a football and covered with sharp green spikes an inch long. As Sibaniel pressed harder and harder on the nose of the durian, it finally surrendered and split open into several sections like an orange.

"You may think what you want about a durian," *Tuan* spoke now, "it is king of all jungle fruit; just be quick and pass it around, Sibaniel."

Sibaniel picked up the split segments of the large fruit and passed them to everyone. Nestled in the white fibrous sections were fat lumps of golden cream. The hungry travelers picked out these lumps with eager fingers and sucked the rich yellow cream from the smooth seeds with exclamations of delight. Durian after durian was opened and disposed of until the last one was finished.

"What a feast! "remarked the Guru. "Nothing could make a better breakfast for us."

Kondima wiped her sticky hands on her skirt and ran them through her hair. Everyone felt better now.

It was another hour before the ridge of the blue mountain was reached. The path led along the saddle for half an hour and emerged finally in a small clearing. Far below, the great ocean lay calm and beautiful as far as the eye could see. Between the mountaintop and

Jungle Thorn

the sea were hills and valleys of lesser height, all covered with living green. It was a breath-taking sight.

Everyone looked at Kondima.

"Is that the valley of water, *Tuan*?" she asked, waving one small hand over the glorious scene. "Oh, how beautiful!" she exclaimed, both hands clasped in ecstacy. "I can see it! I can see it!" A look of relief passed over *Tuan's* thin face. Broad smiles spread over all faces. They stopped to enjoy the enchanting scene for a few minutes, then entered again into deep jungle. The valley of water came no more into view.

The path descended with many steep passages where the travelers had to hold like monkeys to the naked roots of trees.

"You must be very tired, child." *Tuan* swung Kondima to his shoulder and carried her for half an hour. "Just to rest those little legs," he laughed.

At noon they reached a small stream dashing down the mountain through its stony bed. *Tuan* sat down on a large rock. He told Sibaniel to open the *bohongan*, and from its depths he produced a tin of biscuits. Kondima's eyes widened in wonder. The tin was a beauty! How Mookit would like to carry off such a tin! Inside the tin were many shapes and colors of biscuits. Kondima tried quite a few of them. *Tuan* held her on his knee, whispering soft and comforting words to her. She was feeling very far from home and Mother and Chaya and the little mountain village. In fact, although she had enjoyed the trip, she would be glad to see Mookit or Chaya appear out of the forest right now. How happy she would be to go scurrying home with them!

Tuan set her feet in the cool water of the stream. "Play in the water a little," he suggested. "It will rest your tired feet." Sibaniel and the other carrier lolled in the shade with their feet in the stream.

Beyond The Blue Mountain

It was a full hour before they resumed their journey and came at once to the edge of a swamp. Long grass grew in the black mud, and tall trees bent over the boggy ground.

"Ssssh!" *Tuan* put his finger to his lips. All the party stood very still. "See that monkey going down to the swamp to drink?" *Tuan* whispered in Kondima's ear. Following the direction of *Tuan's* pointing finger, Kondima could make out the form of a dark-colored monkey swinging down from a branch of green creeper overhanging a small pool.

"Is there a baby monkey, *Tuan*?" Kondima whispered back. There was indeed. The baby monkey clung to its mother's breast with all four of its tiny hands.

"Oh, *Tuan*! Sibaniel's face froze in horror. He began screaming at the top of his voice. The startled monkey darted up the tree like a flash. Then all of them could see the coils of a great water python and the flash of his blunt head as he made a lunge at the spot where

Jungle Thorn

the monkey had been a second before.

"Let's get out of here!" several voices cried at once. The whole party went trotting along the narrow path by the edge of the swamp at increasing speed until the dangerous ground was at last safely passed.

"I was afraid the snake might have his mate up at this end of the swamp." The Guru puffed a little as they slowed down to a brisk walk.

At the close of the day when the sun was descending in the heavens, they came to a well-beaten path on level ground. Kondima, who had been trotting along with cheerful patience, began to hear strange noises, the like of which she had never heard before. She clutched *Tuan's* hand in real fright. Presently they came out onto a broad place where the ground seemed to be made of stone in a long strip. Right in the middle of this strip stood the strangest animal Kondima had ever seen. It was of a red color and very large, much larger than a water buffalo. It breathed hard and fast and shook a little as it stood there panting in the middle of the smooth rock strip. The beast's eyes were large and set well apart. The whole appearance of the creature was terrible. Kondima looked at the *Tuan*. He appeared to be calm and at ease. He was talking and laughing with a man who rested one hand on the monster. At that moment the animal lifted its voice in a shrill roar. This was too much for the little jungle girl.

She snatched away her hand and went streaking off down the path toward home as fast as her tired legs could carry her, screaming at every jump.

Tuan was a good runner. It was only a few moments until he had Kondima in his arms. "Don't be afraid, little one," he comforted her. "This is our bus, and this is the bus driver. He is a fine fellow. He has a little girl about your size. See, he is going to let us ride on the front

Beyond The Blue Mountain

seat with him." Then the whole party, together with their baggage, was taken aboard the red bus.

Siandoi welcoms Kondima to the house where she and Sibaniel live.

Chapter Six

The House Of Children

*"In that beautiful home He has gone to prepare
For all who are washed and forgiven,
Oh, may we at last find a glad welcome there,
Safe at home in the kingdom of heaven."*

KONDIMA sat very still on *Tuan's* lap during the twenty-five-mile trip into the great city. It seemed a great city to her, for she had never before been beyond the blue mountain.

Kondima had often wished to fly. It would be wonderful to have wings like a bird and fly through the air faster than anything else. Now her wish was more than fulfilled. The red bus flew over the smooth ribbon of rock at a terrifying speed.

Before the journey was ended, Kondima found herself liking it very much. "Oh, won't I have something to tell Chaya and Mookit?" she observed to herself. "I have flown through the air in this red animal which is like a rolling bird. How their eyes will pop when they hear about this!"

It was nearly sundown when the red bus rolled up the street to the *Tuan's* bungalow. Kondima had been so interested in all the motions and noises of the bus that she had taken little time to look at anything else. The bus stopped before a thick green hedge. *Tuan* set her on the ground.

59

Jungle Thorn

Surely this big house couldn't be the home of one family. It must be the council house of a whole village. Then right before Kondima's astonished eyes the doors of the great house opened, and little boys and girls tumbled out and down the steps. They came running toward the red bus. "Oh, Daddy," cried one little boy with yellow curls, "did you bring the little sick girl?"

"Uncle! Uncle! Where is the little girl?" A bright eyed, dark-haired girl raced ahead of the others.

The *Tuan* came forward and knelt with his hand still held by Kondima. The children were upon him immediately. They swarmed over him like eager flies. With much laughing and shouting the group finally composed itself long enough for Kondima to be properly presented. Bennie, Jimmie, and Madge were the *Tuan's* own children. Nancy, June, and Peter were living at the *Tuan's* house. Dorothy and Eileen were the children of the Guru.

"This is Nancy." *Tuan* indicated the gay, eager child who had outrun all the rest. "And this is Bennie," he said as he laid his free hand on the curly head. "This is June." He smiled at a sweet-faced little girl with hazel eyes and brown hair. "Peter is the last of the small fry." *Tuan* laughed as a thin, little dark-haired fellow hid his face behind Bennie with bashful timidity. "Jimmie, Madge, and Bennie call me Daddy; and all the rest call me Uncle." Kondima did not understand but she knew everyone was making her welcome.

"There are more of them, Kondima." *Tuan* had swept the whole group into his arms. "Jimmie is coming out the door right now. He is our big boy. Madge and Dorothy are behind him. They are our big girls." At that moment a fat baby toddled to the window. "That's Eileen." *Tuan* waved a hand toward her.

Kondima was borne along by the eager throng and found herself entering the large living room which was mostly veranda. Two tall, smiling women welcomed the *tuan*s. They must be the *tuan*s' wives, Kondima thought. Since Dorothy held onto the hand of the Guru, that must be his child; and since he went at once to pick up the fat baby, Kondima knew already which were the two little daughters of the Guru. What about the rest of them? None of them looked at all alike, yet some of them must be the *Tuan's* own children.

The *bohongan*s were brought in and taken to the back room; then *Tuan* sat down in an easy chair. He lifted Kondima to one knee and Peter to the other. June climbed on one arm of his chair while Bennie stood on the opposite one. Nancy stood right behind him with both arms about his neck, her merry face radiant with roguish pleasure.

"Daddy, can the little girl's eye get well?" Bennie drew his face into a deep frown. A shudder ran through his small body. "It shivers me and it shakes me to see the little girl's eye."

"Uncle, will you cut the little girl's hair? It is so long and hangs down over her eyes. She can't see at all." It was gentle little June speaking.

"Uncle." Dark-eyed Nancy put her two small hands on both the *Tuan's* cheeks and turned his face toward herself. "Doesn't the little girl have any pretty dresses? Can I give her some of mine? I have so many." Jimmie and Madge had seated themselves on the floor in front of the armchair group. A whole flock of questions were in the making.

"Suppose you all wait and see what happens," he suggested. "Won't that be better than knowing everything all at once?"

Small Peter sighed and sucked his thumb a little. He was in a position of advantage, so he listened and looked from one to another of the children with smiling brown eyes. Kondima nestled closer in the curve of *Tuan's* friendly arm. She was very tired. She could not understand all the children had said, but she knew that all of them were kind and wished her well.

Jungle Thorn

At this moment Sibaniel came in. *"Tuan,"* he said with a big smile, "please allow me to keep the little mountain child at my cottage for the night. She may feel lonesome, and we can speak her language. My wife is waiting for her. Her supper is ready." Then addressing the little girl in her own tongue, he persuaded her to come with him. *Tuan* always talked in Malay, which Kondima understood, but the language of the mountain village was more familiar. She started off with Sibaniel.

"Good night, Kondima," chorused all the children with hearty cheer. *Tuan* rose, putting them all aside.

"You stay here," he commanded. "I must see where Kondima is to spend the night and whether she has a blanket and a mosquito curtain." The tired man followed Sibaniel to his cottage.

"So this is little Kondima. Come to stay with us for a few days?" A beautiful young woman laid her hands on both Kondima's shoulders and looked down at her with kind eyes. On a clean table plates of hot rice stood with bowls of fragrant vegetables and fish. Suddenly Kondima realized that she was starving. Siandoi laughed. Her laugh was like the tone of a silver bell. Kondima had heard such a bell once. A Chinese had brought it to the village. Father said it had likely been stolen from some great house in the city. The laugh of Siandoi reminded her of the bell. A stool was placed for her, and she ate her first meal thus. At home everyone sat on the floor to eat, but the new arrangement did not diminish Kondima's appetite.

Tuan went back to his house and fetched a bright red blanket with a small mosquito curtain. These Sibaniel arranged with a couple of mats into a comfortable bed. it looked inviting, and Kondima tumbled into her blanket under the curtain without a word. She didn't think of crying. She didn't think of Mother, Chaya, Baby Bani, anything. She was fast asleep.

The House Of Children

A clear, sweet voice wakened the mountain child early next morning, but the voice was not speaking to her. She peeked out from the mosquito curtain. Sibaniel and Siandoi were kneeling beside a chair on which rested an open book. Siandoi was praying. She knelt with both hands clasped, her sweet face lifted. Kondima, watching, thought she had never seen anyone so lovely. "She must be like the angels Teacher *Daud* tells us about," thought the little girl. Then drawing the mosquito curtain around her, she too knelt, clasping her hands just like Siandoi. "Dear God, You who can love the little children who are sick and ugly, please love me and make me good."

After breakfast Kondima followed Siandoi to the back of the great house where the clothes were waiting to be washed.

"You go and put on one of my sarongs," Siandoi commanded her. "Then bring me that dirty dress. I will wash it for you. It will be useful for you to have it on the boat." Kondima was back in a few minutes with one of Siandoi's blue sarongs tied high under her arms. The dress she had worn down the mountain was in her hand. Siandoi

Jungle Thorn

took it and put it to soak in a pail of warm soapy water. Then she began pinning the washed clothes to a wire line with small wooden clips. Kondima marveled at the whiteness of the clothes.

"What makes them so white, Siandoi?" she asked.

"Look, Kondima, one must use lots of soap." She held up a thick yellow bar. "One must scrub hard, too, and then they must be rinsed many times in clear water. If they are washed in hot water, it is easier to make them white." The dirty dress was then washed. Siandoi used her best skill on it; and when it hung on the line beside the other clothes, it was remarkably changed in color although still several shades darker than anything else.

"They must have finished breakfast by now," said the gardener's wife as she led Kondima to the door of the big house. Warmhearted Nancy received her with both arms outstretched. Once inside the door she saw many things which had escaped her tired eye the night before. Toys of many strange kinds were scattered about. The two small boys were running a tiny red bus over the floor, sputtering and snorting to make sounds like the real bus.

Kondima watched with fascinated interest. Baby Eileen was building a tower of bright blocks in the corner. Madge and Dorothy were washing dishes in another room where water came out of the wall through a bright thing which would start or stop the water when it was touched by the hand. That was like having a spring in your house.

The tall woman whom Kondima was to call Auntie because the other children did was sitting at a small table. A black whirling thing was on the table. Auntie was pushing cloth through the whirling thing, and it came out sewed together in close, tight stitches not at all like the coarse stitches in Kondima's dress now hanging on the clothesline. The cloth was in small pieces of beautiful bright colors. Nancy and June were sorting the bright pieces from a basket on the

The House Of Children

floor and handing them to Auntie.

"We are making a pillow for you, Kondima," Nancy giggled with delight. "See, it is going to have lots of pretty colors in it. You are going on the big boat to Singapore, and everyone needs a pillow on the boat."

Auntie finished the long rectangle and doubled it together, sewing all around the edge. As she was turning it, Madge came in.

"Here, Madge, you can fill it with kapok and sew up the end." Auntie rose from her place at the small table. "Come, little girl, we are going to wash your hair and make it soft and pretty like Nancy's." She took Kondima by the hand. The little mountain girl had always bathed at the spring on the mountainside. She was much astonished at the conveniences of the bathroom. So intent was she on seeing everything that it was with difficulty the hair got washed. In fact, the other Auntie had to lend a hand before the job was finished off with a good soap bath.

"Now we will just trim up the hair a little," said *Tuan* an hour later when the warm sun and wind on the veranda had thoroughly dried Kondima's hair. He took out his scissors and tied a clean white cloth around her neck. When he had finished, Nancy came running with a mirror. It was the first time Kondima had ever looked in one, and what she saw was so frightening that she hid her face in the folds of *Tuan's* coat and cried for the first time since leaving the little mountain village.

"Come now." *Tuan* took her on his knee, motioning the repentant Nancy away. "Did you see how beautiful your hair looks? It is silky and shiny like Nancy's. Your cheeks are smooth and dimpled, and no child in all the world has a sweeter smile than my little mountain girt. We are going to send you where your eye will be fixed up so it will look nice again."

Jungle Thorn

"Kondima, come with me." Nancy had disposed of the offending mirror and now drew her new friend into the room where the girls slept. She pulled open a drawer and took out a little blue dress. "Let us go to Auntie, and she will try it on you," she said with starry eyes.

The dress was a perfect fit; everyone said so. The children gathered round to admire it. The little ruffled collar lay close to her throat; the puffed sleeves set off her smooth brown arms.

"Oh, what a beautiful dress! Just wait till Mookit sees this! Even Chaya wouldn't know me." Kondima smiled in an embarrassment of pleasure. But this was only the beginning. June came running with a pink dress; and before it was tried on, Nancy was back with a yellow one. All the dresses fit Kondima. She was just the same age and size as the two beautiful little girls who were the *Tuan's* children.

Auntie brought out a packing case and packed six little dresses in it. Then Nancy came with a pair of little white pajamas all speckled with tiny pink rosebuds. Kondima was sure she had never seen

The House Of Children

any garments so beautiful. She wanted to put them on at once and wear them, but Auntie said they had better be saved for the hospital. Some shoes appeared from somewhere and a few pretty handkerchiefs. Madge brought the gorgeous pillow. It, too, was placed in the traveling case. "We will put your red blanket in tomorrow before you go," Auntie said.

It was decided that Kondima should wear a little red-and-white checked dress. Each dress had bloomers of the same material to match it. Kondima rolled Siandoi's sarong up into a tight roll. She smoothed the skirts of the pretty dress. "Am I not one of the *Tuan's* children now?" she asked herself.

Siandoi came in with Kondima's clean dress over her arm. The young woman cried out with delight at the changed appearance of her small friend. Kondima in turn exclaimed over the new look of her old dress.

"You can wear it to sleep in on the boat," Siandoi said.

The rest of the day Kondima played in the big house. The games all took her in. The picture books, the tricycle, the swings, and all the other toys were hers to enjoy and play with as she wished. Kondima was at home. She sensed that this was the house of all children regardless of race or color.

When the children gathered for evening prayers, Kondima sat on *Tuan's* knee, but she could look out and see the full moon rising clear and golden in the sky. The songs of the children rang out with fresh sweetness in the evening air. A twinge of homesickness began to press her heart.

"Uncle, we are making Kondima sad." Nancy patted the little brown hand. "Let's pray now, and then we will play bear."

The game of bear, in which *Tuan* took a leading part, was so exciting that Kondima forgot everything else. When Sibaniel came to

Jungle Thorn

take her to bed, she was laughing and shouting with much hilarity.

"Will there be a house of children like this in Singapore, do you think?" Kondima asked Sibaniel as she held to his hand in the dark.

"Not likely," he answered. "There is no other house like this, but you will find kind people there, and they will make your eye new again. Then you will be as pretty as the little girls in the *Tuan's* house."

"It wasn't because Ellen was pretty that people loved her." Kondima confronted Sibaniel as they stepped into the lighted cottage.

"What are you talking about, child?"

Then Kondima told the gardener and his wife the story of the little girl who had been hit in the face by the stone. Slow, comprehending smiles spread over their faces.

"Yes," Siandoi said as she put both arms around Kondima, "it is not beauty but goodness that makes people loved. We must pray that you will be a good, sweet girl always; then you will be happy, and people will love you, too."

Thus comforted, Kondima lay down to sleep with a prayer and a wish—a prayer that God would make her good and a wish that she might be beautiful.

Siandoi shows Kondima the big ship that goes on the valley of water

Chapter Seven

The Valley Of Water

"Up and away like the dew of the morning,
Soaring from earth to its place in the sun,
Thus may we pass from the world and its toiling
Only remembered by what love has done."

THE FOLLOWING morning Kondima wakened early. "Will I go to Singapore today?" she asked of Siandoi.

"The boat is down there at the wharf." Siandoi laughed. "You will not get on it till this evening, though, so you needn't waken so early."

There was no more sleep for Kondima. She must run with Siandoi to the crown of the hill on which *Tuan's* house stood. Directly below, in the bright blue water lay the ship. In Kondima's sight it was large, and elegant beyond description. The funnel was blue, and tiny figures could be seen climbing its ladders.

"Oh, Siandoi! What would Mookit say? He has never seen a ship. Can it go over the valley of water by itself? Doesn't anything pull it?"

The gardener's wife laughed again at the funny questions the little jungle girl could ask.

"You just wait, Kondima; by tomorrow this time you will know all about ships." They walked back to the big house hand in hand.

As is often the case, once caught in the wonders of busy city life,

Jungle Thorn

Kondima was surprised at nothing any more. Everything was too wonderful. Nothing was impossible. She scrambled into the red bus beside little Eileen that evening without the slightest hesitation. She had completely forgotten her experience of three days before when she had run screaming into the jungle at the first sight of one of these red creatures.

Down on the wharf the ship assumed gigantic proportions. It seemed as big as the world. A trip to the moon or the stars would have been scarcely more fabulous, but Kondima kept her eye on the little traveling case which contained all her new finery, especially the gay pillow and the rosebud pajamas.

It had been arranged by *Tuan* that Kondima should share a cabin with an older Dusun girl named Gar who was going to Singapore for medical attention, and who could speak her dialect. The two became friends at sight. *Tuan* unpacked Kondima's pillow and blanket. After some words of encouragement to both girls, *Tuan* said goodbye and left them to his brother's family.

"Goodbye! Goodbye!" The words floated back as the good ship put out to sea.

"Look, Kondima, *Tuan* has taken off his hat and is waving still!" Sure enough, there was the familiar figure in the khaki suit waving his white sun helmet. The vessel turned and passed behind an island. When it emerged on the distant side, objects on the wharf could no longer be clearly distinguished. Now the Guru, or "Uncle" as Kondima had learned to call him, said that the little ones had better get settled down because the sea was a bit rough. "I will see that you get your supper," he promised as he guided the two Dusun girls to their cabin below.

No one had told Kondima about seasickness.

"I don't want any supper," she whispered when it was brought.

The Valley Of Water

"My head is whirling round and round. I want to go back to the *Tuan's* house. I don't like the valley of water."

Uncle smiled at her. "You will soon get your sea legs, and then you will feel as good as new."

Kondima didn't think she would ever feel good again. She complained to her friend Gar, and the older girl tried to comfort her as best she could, being in the same state of mind herself. The new pillow got a few tears cried onto it. Then Kondima remembered how Siandoi had looked, kneeling with her lovely face uplifted. She remembered the group of singing children in the big house and how they all knelt to pray .at bedtime. She remembered the story of the little girl who was hit by the stone. She lay quiet for a long time. Gar thought her little friend had gone to sleep at last. Then Kondima slipped out of the berth and knelt for a moment by its side. Strangely comforted, she crawled under her new blanket and was sound asleep.

Some time in the night Kondima awoke. For a moment she couldn't think where she was. This was not the little hut on the mountainside or the gardener's house at *Tuan's* place. Then the realization came to her that she was on the ship, the great beautiful ship. It was taking her to Singapore, where she would find powerful medicine for her eye. The great beautiful ship was making hard work of the task.

Kondima felt herself going lower and lower as into a deep valley; then she was tossed up again. Her head felt a sinking sensation as though she were standing on it. Then her feet felt as if they hit the bottom of the berth as she rose again. The great beautiful ship did not smell good.

Dank, moldy odors crept in the door, which was latched partly open. A feeble light came from the hall outside the door. Oh, what a miserable feeling! She turned and braced herself as the good ship plunged and corkscrewed in the rough sea.

There was a small round window over the berth. It was screwed tight shut, but the glass was clear. Kondima got up. She hung onto the heavy screw of the window with one hand and braced herself with the other. Then she looked out. The moon shone overhead; a thousand stars twinkled out of the night, but Kondima did not notice them. She was observing only one thing-the troubled water. The surface of the sea was arranged in hills and valleys. The ship must climb over the hills and descend into each valley between. Frequently one of the hills of water would explode in a wash of white spray and strike the round window a resounding slap. At first Kondima drew back from these in fear, but seeing that not a drop of water entered, she grew bold and laid her face against the cool glass. She enjoyed its smooth moist dampness.

The ship that seemed so great when she climbed aboard seemed but a tiny thing now in the midst of this boundless waste of moving water. How could it ever be found again? It would be lost in all these hills and valleys. No one could see the way.

The Valley Of Water

Was anyone awake on the ship? Kondima slipped out of her berth. She unlatched the door and fastened it again behind her. A heavy rail extended the whole length of the hall. She held onto it to steady herself on the dizzy journey. At last she came to the stairway leading to the upper deck. It was there she had stood the evening before, waving goodbye to *Tuan* and the rest. She climbed the stairs.

The saloon deck was deserted. She walked clear to the end, hanging onto another convenient rail. Then she saw the little ladder leading up. Up—that was where she wanted to go, up and out of this tumbling confusion of turbulent water. She mounted the ladder like a small monkey and stood on the ship's bridge.

There was a room with glass all around it. Inside the room a gray-haired man was bending over some papers spread on a table. In front of the glass room was a great wheel. Another man stood before it, turning it a little every time the ship approached a hill of water. Kondima stood quietly watching the two men.

"These are the drivers of the ship," she convinced herself. "They do not sleep." The gray-haired man smiled as he looked at the papers. "The drivers are not afraid," she encouraged herself. "They do not feel lost." With this comforting assurance she turned and descended the ladder. Her naked feet had just touched the heaving deck when two strong arms caught her.

"What is the child doing climbing about in the middle of the night?" It was a pleasant voice. Kondima turned to see and looked into the face of a sailor. An exclamation of fright broke from his lips. He set her down quietly. Bewildered for a moment, she stood quite still; then she found the stairs, descended to the lower deck, and returned to her cabin. She let herself in and snuggled down to sleep under the red blanket, secure in the knowledge that the drivers of the ship were awake and evidently knew their way.

Jungle Thorn

It was late when Kondima awoke. The steward was standing by her berth. Uncle was with him.

"How is the little mountain girl this morning?" he inquired in a cheerful voice. "We are sailing in smoother waters now. You will feel better today."

The breakfast the steward had brought her looked good. Kondima sat up and tasted it, then finished the bowl of rice gruel and fish. Gar was feeling better, too. The girls looked out of the window. The sea was much smoother now; the waves were very tiny, and the ship plowed through them without rising or falling. To the left, the coast of Borneo was plainly visible. The mountain lay purple against the gray sky, and the green ocean glittered in the sunlight.

Uncle came back after an hour with a large picture book. He laid it in Kondima's lap as she sat cross-legged on the berth.

"This will amuse you, little one," he said. Then opening the book, he pointed to pictures of strange houses, people and flowers, trees and animals such as neither of the girls had seen in all their lives. They spent hours looking at the pictures and wondering about them.

"This animal must be a water buffalo, but his nose drags close to the ground, and his ears are so big! "

"No, it can't be a water buffalo." Gar studied the picture.

"I have heard my father tell of such an animal. It is used by men to lift heavy logs and for riding. My father said they sometimes build little houses and place them on the animal's back. They decorate them with beautiful cloth, and rich people and rajahs ride in them."

"I should like to see such an animal." Kondima regarded it with thoughtful interest. Her eye was tired from looking at pictures so long.

The day had passed quickly, and it was evening again. The sea was calm as a lake.

"We will anchor at midnight and tie alongside at dawn." Uncle

The Valley Of Water

stuck his head in the cabin door after both girls were rolled in their blankets for the night.

"Are we halfway to Singapore, Uncle?" Kondima inquired.

"No, child, but we are going to spend a day loading water buffalo tomorrow."

At midnight Kondima roused from her heavy sleep enough to be aware of a great stillness. The throb of the engine had ceased. In the silence she heard the sound of a heavy chain running through iron. Then all was quiet.

The girls wakened at dawn with the noise of activity everywhere. They pressed their faces against the small window. There was a town visible in the background, and in the foreground was a wharf of heavy planks with large iron knobs set in the edge. Great loops of heavy cable were fastened around the knobs, and the ship was slowly drawing nearer to the wharf.

Kondima put on her new blue dress and ascended with Gar to the deck where they could watch the loading. Already the wharf was alive with pushing, shouting coolies. Piles of rubber and bales of merchandise were stacked about. The noise of machinery could be heard from the front of the ship. A long metal arm swung out over the wharf. A great iron hook dangled from the end of it. A man snatched the hook and fastened it in a bale of merchandise on the wharf. Then the giant arm raised the bale and swung it over the side of the ship, depositing it gently on the deck. Busy workers rolled it away.

"How does the arm know when to turn?" asked Kondima of Gar. "What makes the hook go up and down?"

"Go up forward and see for yourself," answered Gar, who had long ago become discouraged trying to answer Kondima's questions.

"It is a man who does it," she informed her friend when she returned. "The man thinks, and the arm and the hook do the work."

Jungle Thorn

At noon the loading of the water buffalo began. A herd of them was driven onto the wharf. The heavy hook swung out overhead. A band of heavy canvas was passed under the body of a buffalo cow. The two ends of the band were strong loops. These were passed over the hook which was lowered to the level of the animal's back. Then the hook began to move upward. The band tightened around the frightened buffalo. Her feet left the wharf, and she flew into the air. The great arm swung her, bellowing and kicking, over the deck, then let her carefully down into the hold. One by one the great animals were loaded. Kondima exclaimed to Gar, "How silly they are! They should be glad to have a fine flying ride like that." A memory stirred in her mind; and she added, "Of course, I suppose they never saw a ship or a hook before; so perhaps we shouldn't blame them."

The following day the sea was rough again. Neither of the girls wanted to leave their berths to see the water buffalo unloaded at Miri. That evening when the boat sailed from the Miri anchorage, she headed straight west, and soon the mountains of Borneo were left behind. There was nothing to be seen in any direction but endless waves of troubled water.

Three days later the good ship anchored in Singapore harbor. Kondima felt that she had seen a good deal of the world, but one glimpse of the busy streets of that truly great city gave her the feeling she had the first time she saw the red bus. This time there was no place to run. She held tightly to the hand of Uncle. Dressed in her pretty yellow dress, wearing shoes for the first time in her life, Kondima was whisked away by motor car to the sunny compound where Uncle and his family lived. Gar was taken with them.

On the following morning Uncle, true to his promise, took both girls to the General Hospital and made all arrangements for their care.

The Valley Of Water

Gar was sent to the women's ward and Kondima to the children's ward. They did not see each other again.

Kondima's bed in the hospital ward was close to the wall.

Chapter Eight

The House Of Sickness

"Heavenly truth that in life we have spoken,
Beautiful seed that on earth we have sown;
These shall pass onward when we are forgotten,
Fruits of the harvest and what love has done."

D OCTOR, come and see the little girl from the Borneo mountains."
Kondima was sitting cross-legged on the high white bed. A
pleasant-faced nurse was standing over her. It was the nurse who had
spoken. A tall, sandy haired doctor stepped to the nurse's side.

"So this is the child"—he twisted his mustache—"looks a little
thin, Nurse; give her lots of milk and anything else you can to fatten
her up a little."

"The eye looks terrible, doesn't it?" The nurse tipped the child's
head back so the doctor could see.

"It does, it does, but we will fix that." The good man reached in
his pocket and took out a gumdrop. He popped it into the open mouth
of Kondima. She had listened to the conversation and had heard every
word, but the gumdrop spoke a language she could understand better.

The doctor and the nurse spoke in English. "Ah, what a smile this
little one has!" the doctor exclaimed as he turned on his heel and continued with his round of patients.

Jungle Thorn

This was Kondima's first morning in the house of sickness. Her bed was one of many. The beds stood in two long rows down the length of a long room, and there was a sick child in every bed. Few of them could sit up like Kondima. Some had white cloth wrapped around their legs or arms. In the bed next to Kondima was an Indian child. She was so thin that even her bones seemed to have shrunk, and Kondima never looked at her without thinking of a spider. On the other side was the white wall, for Kondima's bed was the last in the row.

Nurse looked kindly at the new patient. "You will be here for several weeks, child," she said. "We are going to try to help you all we can, and you must help us and do just what the doctor says so that you may get well soon." The nurse spoke in Malay. Kondima understood. She nodded her head and smiled again.

When Kondima's noon meal was brought, she stared in surprise at the tray. The jolly Chinese boy who fetched it smiled and jabbered talk Kondima could not understand. He pointed to a large round thing on the tray. She picked up the object and looked at it. It was a beautiful red color and smooth as a baby's cheek.

It had a deep dimple in the top from which a small stem stuck out.

"This must be fruit." Kondima turned the ball around in her small hands. A sharp knife lay on the plate that held the fruit. "Should I cut it, I wonder?" She replaced the beautiful thing with care. "I will ask Nurse about it. Such a pretty thing may be to look at instead of for eating."

There were other strange things on the tray. There was a tall glass full of white water. "That must be what Teacher *Daud* bought for his puppy; it looks the same." She drank a little. It tasted slightly sweet. In a little white pan was something golden and brown. Kondima stuck her finger in and tasted the soft stuff. It was sweet, too, and something like the cream of the durian fruit, but not so good. On a large plate were more familiar foods—potatoes, vegetables, and

The House Of Sickness

a breast of chicken. On another plate were some strange biscuits, square and porous looking. Beside them was a square of yellow.

Beginning on the familiar foods, Kondima began to eat. Before she had finished, a young nurse stopped beside her bed. "How is our little girl getting on?" she inquired with a smile. "The doctor wants you to eat everything on your tray. He wants to see you getting plump and healthy."

Kondima held up the large red fruit. "What is it?"

"Of course, you never saw one before. That is called an apple. It is very good for you. Doctor has said that you must have one every day."

"Will I have another one tomorrow?" Kondima questioned, almost speechless with delight.

"Yes, every day. Now be sure to drink your milk." She pointed to the glass of what looked like white water.

After the nurse had gone, Kondima cut the red fruit in two. There were small brown seeds in the middle. "I wonder if they would grow in our village." She picked them all out and tied them in the corner of her handkerchief. She removed almost all the center of the apple this way. Then she sliced off a very thin slice and ate it. The apple was good. It was not so good as durian, but better than almost anything else she had ever tasted. She ate it all. It was very good. That afternoon a nurse came to Kondima's bed with a small, white pan and a bottle with some fluffy stuff in a blue paper. "We are going to wash your eye with some medicine," she explained.

Kondima braced herself. It would hurt, she knew, but had she not come to the big city for this? Had she not traversed the long trail down from the mountain village? Had she not sailed in the great ship over the valley of water just for this medicine? She bore the treatment without flinching and without a whimper.

Nurse was surprised. "So you can smile after that?" She patted the smooth dark hair tenderly. "You are a brave little girl." It was the good left eye that had received the treatment.

For weeks Kondima's left eye was treated with medicine. The good doctor found that she had worms and malaria. She ate medicine for these afflictions. No matter what medicine was offered, no matter what treatment prescribed, she accepted it as a benefit and a gift with such gratefulness that the doctor and nurses often turned from her bed with misty eyes.

Every day people came to see the little girl who had journeyed so far. Uncle and his family came often. They brought pictures and flowers and news from the *Tuan's* great big house across the valley of water.

One day a young intern came. He brought a big parcel. "Open it, Kondima," he insisted. She took the parcel in both hands, turning it over and looking at it from all sides. Slowly she took off all the strings, loosening each one and winding the string into a ball. Then she removed the paper with care, folding it with graceful fingers. At last she lifted the cover.

"Oh, really—truly dishes! Just like at the *Tuan's* house!" She clapped her hands for joy. She took out a tiny cup and held it in her

The House Of Sickness

little brown hand. She rubbed the smooth surface against her cheek.

"Do you like it, little girl?"

The child took one of his hands in both of hers and looked up at him with one lighted eye.

After that whenever the young intern came to the children's ward, he brought out something for Kondima; so did many of the nurses and attendants.

"I declare I'll have to use a whole locker for the child's trinkets," said the nurse as she drew a couple of new packages from under Kondima's bed.

One of the parcels had contained a beautiful doll, latest gift of the young intern. The box was empty; the doll was in Kondima's arms, learning the soft language of the mountains which no one else in the children's ward could talk. Kondima bent over her new baby. The

Jungle Thorn

dolly's eyes were brown, and her hair was black. Her cheeks were smooth and rosy.

"She looks like Nancy," thought the little girl. "She looks like I would like to look." She heaved a heavy sigh. After a thoughtful silence she spoke aloud. "I will call her name Ellen so I will always remember."

Finally there came a day when Kondima was wheeled away to surgery. She clutched the sides of the table. "They are going to take out my bad eye," she said to herself. "It will hurt, but this is what I came for. How much better my face will look with that terrible eye gone." She saw a white object above her face and smelled a peculiar odor. Then all things faded from her sight. Later when Kondima woke in her own bed, she could see nothing at all. Had the white doctor taken away both her eyes? She tried to lift her hand.

"Lie still, little girl." It was the voice of her favorite nurse. "You are all right now. There is a bandage over both your eyes, and you will not be able to see for a few days, but you will have a nice time. Here is your dolly; you may talk to her." Kondima lay for a long time with little Ellen in her arms. Slowly the great drowsiness passed away. The

The House Of Sickness

little girl of long ago had come to life again in her arms, the same little girl whose pretty face the cruel stone had ruined. Now she was all well and beautiful. She would live with Kondima always and never be sad or lonely any more.

"When we go home," she whispered, "you will have to ride up the mountain in the *bohongan*, but you won't mind that. I will walk right beside you, and you will hear my voice talking all the time." She shifted the doll to the other arm. "You will see Mother and Father and Chaya and Mookit and Baby Bani and all the village people, and you will see my other baby who is waiting for us there. I will wash your clothes myself and keep you clean just like the nurses in this hospital, and you will sleep with me every night."

Those who passed by the bed of the little girl with a bandage over both eyes remarked that they never heard her cry. They had never heard her complain, and the sweetest smile in the hospital was worn by the little girl from the Borneo mountains.

On the day when the bandage was removed, half the ward staff were standing about. It was evening, and the sandy-haired surgeon declared that he had been forced to elbow his way clear in from the street to see his now-famous patient. The horrible ruined eye was gone. The other eye looked straight into the kind surgeon's face.

"Now, Kondima"—he turned her face away from the light—"your eye is as bright and twinkling as a star. The infection is all gone. In a few days we will fit you with a new glass eye that will look so like your own you can hardly tell the difference."

When the doctor had gone, Kondima reached up an inquiring hand. Sure enough, the bad eye was gone. The lid drooped over an empty socket. With a sigh of content she snuggled Ellen in her arms and slept.

In the morning she tried to remember what the doctor had said.

Jungle Thorn

But she understood only a few of the words in the language of these white people. She did not understand that she was to have a new eye. It was enough that the old ruined eye was gone. A closed eye was not entirely satisfactory, but it was at least nothing frightful to look at. A deep thankfulness filled her heart. Everyone in the hospital was good. How kind they had been! She could only smile her thanks and grateful affection on them all.

Kondima's traveling case was under her bed. She had worn some of the little dresses on the great ship; but Auntie, the new Auntie, had laundered them all. She packed them again in the traveling case so all would be ready when Kondima would be permitted to leave the hospital.

"How about these pretty pajamas?" Nurse then held them up. "Would you like to wear them to call on the doctor?"

Kondima sat up instantly. She took off the hospital gown and put on the rosebud pajamas. Nurse took her hand and led her down the long ward to the far end, then down some steps to a great door. Inside the door was a pleasant room, and beyond it was a smaller room where the sandy-haired doctor waited.

"Just sit here." He lifted Kondima to a tall stool. He turned her face up toward his and studied it for a long time. Then he took a large shallow box and set it on a table. It contained a number of glass balls. As he looked at them, he hummed a funny little tune. He took one ball and held it close to Kondima's good eye, then put it back. He did this several times.

"Look, Nurse," he finally said, "this is perfect!" He dipped the glass ball in some fluid, lifted the lid where the bad eye had been, and popped the glass ball in.

"There now, little one." He stood off smiling and rubbing his hands together with great satisfaction. "What a pretty child you are!"

The House Of Sickness

Nurse stepped into the next room and returned holding a mirror. Kondima looked in the glass. Was it really she herself? A pretty little girl with two clear brown eyes looked back at her. She clapped her hands, "Is it me? It can't be!"

Nurse and Doctor laughed and appeared in every way delighted.

There were many things Kondima wanted to say, but the words died on her lips. She couldn't make the doctor understand. She took his hand in both hers and laid it against her cheek.

"What kind people!" she said to herself. "Even in this house of sickness the kindness of people makes it beautiful."

Kondima looked through the porthole from her cabin on the ship.

Chapter Nine

Into The Sunrise

"Author of love, when Thou callest Thy jewels,
When the bright crowns of rejoicing are won,
May we be numbered among Thy disciples
Who are remembered for what love has done."

KONDIMA leaned hard on the heavy brass screw that held the port window shut. It slowly swung back, and she pulled the round window open. The fresh breath of the late darkness swept her face as she leaned out the window, resting both arms on the cool copper of the window's wide flange.

The eastern horizon was brushed with the faintest pink of dawn. She looked down at the water. The splash of innumerable small wavelets against the dark iron hull of the ship created an illusion of tremendous speed. The stars still lingered in the morning sky, but close at hand the mountainous island of Gaya loomed dark and mysterious.

"We are almost there," Kondima mused to herself. She counted on her fingers, "One—two—three—four—five—six. It has been six days since Uncle put me on the boat. Now I am almost home. Now I will see *Tuan* and his children. I will show them all the beautiful things the people at the hospital gave me. I will see Siandoi. How her eyes will

Jungle Thorn

shine when I tell her about all the people and all the strange things in Singapore."

The mist closed in and shut out the rosy promise of dawn. The land and the stars disappeared, but Kondima knew that just around Gaya Island lay the Jesselton wharf. It would be only a few minutes now until the "Densamud" would drop her anchor off the jetty. Kondima still hung in the open porthole, straining her eye to catch a glimpse of something that would confirm and assure her that the long journey was nearly done.

"Tomorrow I will go home to the village." She clasped both hands and leaned her chin on them. "It will take a big *bohongan* to carry all my things. How Mookit's eyes will pop when he sees my Ellen baby!" She drew her head in and lifted the doll from her place under the red blanket. "I will always love you, my little Ellen; but I will love my other baby, too. I will love you both the same. It is love that makes people the same." Kondima pondered over this great new thought for a long time. Was it not love that made all the children of equal importance at the *Tuan's* house? Was it not love for all manner of people, both good and bad, that made everyone the same in God's sight? So love for her two dollies would make them of equal value to their owner. One was beautiful and one was ugly, but her love for them would be the same.

"I will call my other dolly *Intan* because that means 'treasure,' and then Mookit will know that having a beautiful dolly from the great city has not made me forget my first baby."

The great ship was moving slower and slower. Then it stopped altogether. The throb of the engines ceased, and the rattle of the anchor chain signified that all was at rest, and the good ship awaited the break of day which was drawing on with weavings of light through the purple mist.

Into The Sunrise

Kondima snuggled under her blanket and lay quietly for a few minutes. She was wide awake; who could sleep on such an important morning as this one? Presently she heard the noise of the winches as the ship drew alongside the wharf and made fast its cables. Then she scrambled out of her berth. She opened her traveling case and drew out her rosebud pajamas. Surely no other attire could be so suitable for this great occasion. All her other possessions were carefully packed in the case and in the large parcel which stood inside the cabin door. Uncle had wrapped it and roped it, and Kondima had not touched it since leaving Singapore. Now she began tugging at it with all her strength. Just how she was to get her traveling case and the great parcel out onto the deck was not at all clear to her. She opened her door slowly and quietly and looked out. "Well, little lady, so it's you again." A friendly sailor stopped and looked inquiringly into her face. "So it's you—you." He stroked his chin and seemed to be in deep thought. "Ah, yes, now I remember where I saw you—thought that face looked familiar. What have they done to that awful-looking eye of yours?"

Kondima backed into the cabin.

"Is that great bundle in there yours?" he asked. Kondima nodded.

"How are you going to take it off the ship? Here, coolie." He motioned to a Chinese coming down the narrow hall. "Take that parcel out for the little missy. Be quick, too. I think someone is waiting for her on the wharf." He picked up Kondima's traveling case and, taking her by the hand, ascended to the saloon deck, from whence a ladder ran down to the wharf. Kondima caught a quick look out over the ship's rail, and her heart gave a great leap of joy. There on the wharf was *Tuan* with Nancy and Madge. The sailor caught her in his strong arms and raced down the ladder like a monkey.

"Here, my friend," the sailor man addressed *Tuan*, "this young lady gave me one of the biggest frights of my life on our trip out about

93

four months ago. I see she is all well and beautiful again, and it gives me great pleasure to turn her over bag and baggage. She has given me three beautiful smiles, and I will accept them in payment for the awful scare she gave me."

Tuan laughed and looked down at her with deep satisfaction in his gray eyes. "So they have made you beautiful." He held her off at arm's length and looked her over. "They have certainly fed you well. You are as fresh and as plump as the day rose in our garden. The eye is perfect, and the smile is the same, none sweeter in the Borneo mountains."

Madge and Nancy were dancing with joy and surprise. They had recognized the rosebud pajamas, and this made Nancy bubble over with happiness. They drew Kondima with them.

"But, no!"—she stopped short—"my parcel must come, too."

Tuan's eyes opened in surprise, and both Madge and Nancy cried out with astonishment.

"Does this really belong to you?" *Tuan* asked. "Yes, of course." Kondima ran to the big bundle and laid hold of it as though she would carry it home single-handedly. "These are the gifts the kind people at the hospital gave me."

A wave from the sailor on the deck reassured *Tuan*, and he directed the coolie to carry the bundle to the red bus waiting at the end of the pier. They all followed and were soon happily on their way up the hill to the house of children.

June and Bennie, Peter and Jimmie, Siandoi and Sibaniel—they all ran out to welcome the dear wanderer back again. Kondima felt the cozy warmth of the great house, and its huge family enveloped her like a soft garment.

"Oh, what a nice new eye! "Siandoi clasped her hands as she always did at prayer.

"Uncle, Kondima is pretty now," said June as she tugged at one of *Tuan's* big hands.

"Daddy, Daddy, why does the little girl wear her pajamas in the daytime?" Bennie looked puzzled.

"She likes them the best of all her clothes." Nancy preened herself with great satisfaction.

So Kondima came back to the house of children. The rejoicing was so general that *Tuan* declared they must have a feast to celebrate the home-coming and the restoration of their little Kondima. Auntie, Siandoi, and Madge made ready a delicious repast of red rice, curry, fried bananas, and several kinds of vegetables. Bennie and Nancy requested that the feast be eaten out of doors, so it turned out to be a joyous picnic under the trees.

After the meal was over and the dishes were washed, Kondima announced, "Now I am going to show you all the things I got in Singapore."

Tuan set the heavy parcel in the middle of the veranda and cut the heavy cords. Kondima removed the wrappings with some help from a number of small, eager hands. Two large cartons were revealed. Each one contained a number of bundles and boxes. There were picture books, big and little, thick and thin; also games of many kinds, a beautiful set of dishes, a whole fleet of small buses and motor cars, trucks and trams. Kondima laughed at these, remembering her terrible fright at first sight of the red bus.

Several boxes were sealed and contained delicious biscuits. "I learned to eat those in the hospital," she said. "Mookit and Alijah and Chaya never saw any; I guess they will be surprised."

"Yes, I think they will." *Tuan* looked a little bewildered by all this sudden wealth that had come to his little Kondima.

A family of Teddy bears next appeared from the depths of the carton, together with a white horse, an elephant, a duck on wheels, and a whole menagerie of small glass and china animals packed in cotton. Kondima could name every one of them.

"Now I will show you my baby." Kondima opened her traveling case and drew out the dolly. "Her name is Ellen." She looked at *Tuan*. "She is good and beautiful, and I love her and take good care of her." She cuddled the doll in her arms while all the children drew near to touch Ellen's dark curls and rosy cheeks.

"You may play with all my things." Kondima still held the dolly in her arms, but she nodded generously toward the whole assortment of toys on the floor.

Into The Sunrise

"No, no!" *Tuan* spoke with sudden decision as he started packing all the toys back in their boxes. "No, I think these should all be put back at once. There will be plenty of little folk in Durian village to play with all these things; and I hope, Kondima, that you will be generous with them, too."

After the toys were all packed again, and *Tuan* had gone back to his office to his papers and books, Bennie and Jimmie invited all the little girls to come out and see their pet monkey ride the dog for a horse.

Pixie was a tiny black monkey; and Captain, the dog, was a large black-and-white mongrel who loved children and monkeys, too. The tiny monkey sat on the big dog's back holding tight to his long hair, and the dog raced back and forth on the long cement walk, with the monkey screaming and hissing like a professional rider. The children laughed until they could laugh no more.

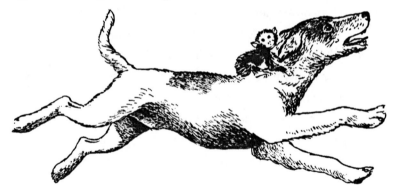

"Look!" cried Bennie, pointing down where the walk ended at a curve of the hill. "Look, there comes Teacher *Daud*." Sure enough, there was the native teacher from the mountain village striding up the hill.

His face relaxed into broad smiles as he drew near the group of waiting children. He had recognized Kondima. It was not easy, for her

97

Jungle Thorn

appearance had changed greatly; but her merry laugh was the same, and besides he was expecting her to be there.

"Kondima, child, how well you look!" the young teacher exclaimed as he took the child by the hand and looked down at her with happiness shining out of his kind face. "Your eye is as good as ever, and you are so rosy and fat your mother won't know you." Kondima and the other children followed *Daud* into *Tuan's* office. The missionary looked up from his papers in surprise and laid everything aside to talk with this visitor from Durian village.

"I am glad to see Kondima here," began the young man. "Her mother is very anxious about her. She has been away over four moons already, and the heathen people in the village are saying that she will never come back any more." He looked at Kondima with a satisfied smile and added, "I am sure that when they see her, they will forget all the long time of waiting for joy that she is well again."

Then the two men fell to talking of the people in the village. All the news was of great interest to Kondima, who leaned on *Tuan's* knee and listened eagerly. Old Kokit was needing more of the rubbing medicine. The heavy rains had made his bones ache more than usual. Gooloon and his wife were listening to the teaching every day now, but they still kept the largest herd of pigs in the village; and it seemed hard for them to give up the dirty animals.

"Is my mother well?" Kondima asked as she looked up into *Daud's* face.

"Of course, my child, I should have told you at once your mother is well, and there is a new baby brother waiting for you when we go back to the village tomorrow. You will like that. Chaya is a good girl. She can cook and pound rice and work in the field just like a grown woman. Bani is a big fellow; he talks a lot and runs all over the village."

Into The Sunrise

"Kondima, will you go home with Teacher *Daud* tomorrow?" Bennie inquired with grave interest.

"Kondima must go home as quickly as possible." *Tuan* lifted the child to his knee. "We have kept her too long already, but some day she will come back, and perhaps we will have a nice school where lots of boys and girls can come and learn many useful things."

Kondima pins a rose on the *bohongan.*

Chapter Ten

Magic Beyond Magic

*"Song of all songs till we pass the bright portal,
Theme of all themes when we gather on high,
Joy of all joys through the ages immortal
Christ and His love as the glad years roll by."*

THE DAY ROSE beside Siandoi's cottage was opening pure and white in the early dawn when Teacher *Daud* and Kondima slipped away into the morning. The rose would be pink at noon and red by sundown. Kondima picked one of the white blossoms and fastened it onto the *bohongan* where all her possessions were packed for traveling.

"The rose is just like this day is going to be," Kondima thought to herself. "It will get brighter and more beautiful every hour."

"Good-by, little one." *Tuan* turned Kondima's face up to his as he had done that night in the village when he first saw the injured eye. "Your face is sweet and beautiful again, and you are clean and healthy. Be careful to keep clean and to be a good, obedient girl. I will be up the mountain one of these days." *Tuan* sighed.

"Why do you sigh?" asked *Daud*. "This is a wonderful thing that has been donel The village people will be astonished, and the parents will be beside themselves with joy."

Jungle Thorn

"I know, I know." *Tuan* laid his hand on the young man's shoulder. I was not thinking of that; I was thinking of the thousands of little ones who suffer such terrible hurts with no one to relieve their pain." Then the smiles came back to the gray eyes, and he walked with them to the curve of the hill.

"Are we nearly there?" It was the hundredth time Kondima had asked the eager question.

"Do you see that green hill with the great tree standing higher than all the others?" *Daud* had deposited the *bohongan* by the side of the path, and now he pointed far across the valley. "That's home!"

Kondima looked at the distant hill. "Come on, let's hurry; I want to get there before sundown." So saying, she scampered along so briskly that *Daud* marveled at her tireless energy. All day long she had been running ahead of him.

"What kind of medicine did they give you in Singapore?" he asked finally. "I never saw a child who could run up a mountain like you have today."

Kondima laughed as *Daud* puffed along under the weight of the laden *bohongan*. "I guess they cured me of all my sicknesses, and it just feels good inside me. I want to run and laugh and, of course, I want to see Father and Mother and Chaya and Bani and the new baby."

The travelers had come to the edge of the clearing where the path emerged from the jungle before anyone discovered them. Then there was a great shout raised.

"Kondima comes! Kondima comes!" Mookit was running through the village like a wild thing, screeching the news to everyone. In an instant the village was alive. Men, women, and children tumbled from every door and raced one another up the hill.

Kondima had waited long for this moment. *Daud* seemed to sense

Magic Beyond Magic

its importance and lowered the *bohongan*. The two stood waiting while the eager throng rapidly approached.

"Wonderful! Wonderful! "they exclaimed in loud voices as they crowded round Kondima. "Look, the awful eye is completely cured. It is as good as new! Wonderful! Wonderful!"

Mother burst into tears, Chaya danced with joy, and Mookit bounced here and there and everywhere yelling for no reason at all. The amazement of the village knew no bounds. It was better than any of them had dared to hope.

"Oh, see her beautiful clothes! "shouted Alijah. "I never saw such clothes before. Do all the *Tuan's* children wear such things?"

"How fat you are! "screamed Kokit's daughter.

"They must have given you the best rice in the world." Everyone talked in a loud voice. They were so excited they seemed to have a need for yelling in order to reassure themselves that the things they were seeing were actually real and not some dream of magic.

"What is in the *bohongan*?" Mookit's mother asked. "Have you got more clothes in there?"

Kondima stood in the midst of the shouting company, calm and with a feeling of pure delight. They felt of her plump arms. They turned up the hems of her pajama trousers. They stroked her hair. They pinched her cheeks, and most of all they examined with keenest interest her new eye.

"Can you see out of your eye as well as you ever did?" inquired one of the village fathers. For answer the little girl lifted her hand to her eye and with a quick movement flipped it out, holding it in her extended hand for everyone to see.

The astonished villagers fell back in consternation, knocking one another over in their fright. This was magic beyond magic. It was too much! Kondima's merry laughter rang out loud and clear in the

Jungle Thorn

evening air. The roguish Kondima laughed until the tears ran from her good left eye.

Mookit was the first to recover himself. As he again ventured to draw near to this miracle of miracles, she slipped the eye back into place again.

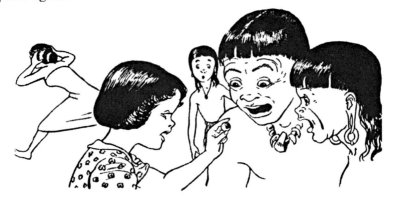

"Kondima, do that to your other eye," he commanded. At this Kondima laughed again. The good folk again drew around her, and together the whole glad company descended to the village.

That was an evening nobody in Durian village ever forgot. There was not room in the home of Kondima's father for all the people to gather, so *Daud* asked all of them to come over to his cottage. By much crowding they managed to get in. There were many questions asked, but the contents of the *bohongan* were the center of interest for all the small folk of the village. As each toy was removed from the package, Kondima had a story to tell about it. With great amusement she told of her fright at the first sight of the red bus.

"This little girl is very tired," Teacher *Daud* explained to the excited villagers. "I think we should all go home to bed, and another day will come tomorrow; then we can hear more about Kondima's travels.

"Chaya"—the two girls had crawled under their mosquito curtain after the new baby had been properly admired and cuddled—"Chaya, is my dolly that Mookit gave me still tied to the beam?" Chaya crept out from under the curtain and scrambled up to the high beam from which she untied the precious bundle and delivered it safely to its owner.

Kondima had taken the dolly Ellen in her arms. With great tenderness she gathered the other baby to her breast.

"Surely you don't want that old ugly thing now that you have the nice new baby from the city." Chaya eyed the wooden doll with great distaste.

"I love them both the same." Kondima held the dollies close. "God loves all His children the same, and so do I." She laid them down side by side and drew a corner of the red blanket over them. "*Tuan* loved me when my eye looked so terrible and even the sailor on the great boat was so frightened of me that he cried out like Mookit does when he is scared."

The two girls and the two dollies snuggled down to sleep.

Early the following morning Kondima took a large bar of yellow soap and a bundle of clothes in a flat basket and went down to the spring. Two or three of the most energetic women of the village were there already. With amused smiles they watched Kondima spread her small garments on the flat washing rock and begin to scrub and beat vigorously. She paid no heed to their watchful attention, but kept steadily at her task until the small pile of dresses and the rosebud pajamas were as clean and fresh as they could possibly be made. She looked admiringly at them. "Even Siandoi could not wash them cleaner," she assured herself. Returning to the hut, she fetched a length of rattan and fastened it between a corner of the hut and the durian tree. On this she hung the washed garments.

Mookit came to watch this last part of the washing. He even helped a little with the fastening of the rattan clothesline. "You are very clever to think of drying your clothes like this," he said thoughtfully. "If you tried to dry them on the grass, the pigs would probably eat them up."

"It seems to me there are more pigs than ever before." Kondima eyed one of the razorback swine which, as usual, were roaming at will all about the village. "There has been a big fight about the pigs." Mookit became confidential. "Gooloon has got more than anyone else, and they all say that they will not get rid of their pigs unless he does."

Every morning after that found Kondima at the spring with her personal washing. She remembered how the white uniforms had looked in the hospital. She remembered Siandoi and her beautiful washings

Magic Beyond Magic

drying on the hill at the house of children. In her stout little heart she resolved that she would never be dirty again. The village folk laughed at her. "Who sees you, Kondima, to make you so particular about your clothes?" they asked.

"I can see myself," she answered rather tersely.

Kondima had grown so plump on her long trip to the great city that she was scarcely smaller than Chaya. "I wonder if you can wear my new dresses, too," Kondima remarked generously as she folded away her clean washing. So she tried one of them on her sister. It was a little short, but the happy smiles of Chaya and the warm contentment in Mother's eyes settled the matter. Kondima gave Chaya half of her clothes, but she reserved the rosebud pajamas for herself.

Mookit was rewarded with a book, a kaleidoscope, the stuffed elephant, and a small red bus. He had never imagined such wealth and became Kondima's devoted slave from that day forward.

Alijah was not forgotten, and Baby Bani could be seen any day running small trucks and motor cars over the rough floor of the hut, having been instructed by Kondima as to the proper noises of sputtering and snorting that went with the motion of such toys.

All the village was richer for the visit of Kondima to Singapore. *Daud* remarked, "She is the lesson book from which all the people are willing to read."

"Elder sister." It was Kondima's voice calling at the door of Kokit's daughter.

"Come in, child." The young woman greeted Kondima with kindness and affection. She sat down cross-legged on the mat with Kokit's daughter and watched with intelligent interest as she slowly fashioned a winnowing basket from strips of bamboo.

"Tell me, Kondima," began the young woman, "what kind of medicine did they use to make your eye well again?"

Jungle Thorn

"They made me go to sleep; and when I woke up, the bad eye was gone, and then after a long time they put the new eye in where the old one had been." Kondima then related the marvels of the great hospital in Singapore, which were always wonderful to the listeners in the mountain village.

"Do you remember how I have always hated the white man's medicine?" Kondima nodded. Kokit's daughter then said earnestly, "I am sure now that the stories I have heard about it are false."

"Will you follow the Jesus teaching, elder sister?" asked Kondima. "It is Jesus who makes the people in the hospital so kind. It is Jesus who makes the *Tuan* kind. It is Jesus who makes the house of children happy, and I believe He can make any house bright and happy."

Then Kondima told Kokit's daughter of the beautiful Siandoi and how she clasped her hands and knelt every morning and evening to pray. She told of the clean and cheerful little cottage. The bamboo strips lay neglected as the daughter of Kokit listened.

"It is the pigs," she finally said. "My husband Gooloon loves the pigs, and he will not give them up. If it were not for the pigs, we could follow the Jesus teaching; but with the pigs around, we are always dirty, and we cannot be clean people."

That night Chaya and Kondima lay awake for a long time trying to think of some plan to rid the village of the pigs, but both girls fell asleep without reaching any decision. After all, what could two small girls do against a hundred pigs?

Chapter Eleven

Lost And Found

"Perish forever the world and its pleasures,
Better the trust of the poor and unknown,
Blessed the man who in tender remembrance
Lives in our hearts for the love he has shown."

THE WEEKS fled away with measured swiftness, and the rice planting season came again. It had been a long time since *Tuan* had visited the village, but it was rumored among the mountain people that he had moved out of the city and was establishing a new school right at the end of the bus line where the long trail down the mountain ended in a paved road. It was near the very spot where Kondima had her terrible fright over the red bus.

Kondima had not seen the *Tuan* and his children for a long time. She often thought of them with a warm tugging at her heart. Memories of the house of children and all the joyful activity there filled her with a vague loneliness she could feel, but could not express. She was growing fast now; and the little dresses, although still clean and fresh, were getting so short and tight that she could no longer wear them with comfort. Often she put on the long black skirt and short light jacket that was the ordinary dress of the village girls.

"Kondima, Chaya, we are all going to the rice field today." Mother

Kondima wearing her village clothes after she came home

Lost And Found

shook the two girls awake in the early morning light and spoke to Kondima. "Chaya must go with us, for there is much work to be done today. We will take the babies along so that you may gather firewood today. We will be back at sundown, and you must have the rice cooked for us so we may eat our supper.

Chaya tumbled out of the mosquito curtain at once and began picking up things and putting them in a big basket. Mother roused the small boys and strapped the smaller one to Chaya's back. After tying Bani on her own back, the mother, with the rest, left for the distant clearing in the jungle.

Kondima turned over on her mat. She hugged her two dollies close and adjusted the loved pillow. "Bother the old firewood," she thought savagely. "Why do I have to work so hard?" she sniffed with injured dignity. Not being able to compose herself to sleep again, she arose, took the big water bamboos to the spring, and filled them. As she returned, Mookit came out of his house looking very sleepy.

"Where are you going, Mookit?" she demanded.

"Father says I must dig a ditch back of the house this morning to drain the water away from the hen roost." Mookit yawned and loitered by the ladder of his house.

"I am leaving," said Kondima. "I am tired of being worked to death, what with carrying water and wood and babies and cooking—I have decided not to stay here any longer."

Mookit's round eyes almost dropped out of his head. "Where will you go, Kondima?" He sat down on the ladder to listen to her answer.

"I will go to the *Tuan's* house," she exclaimed. "After all, I am one of his children, and he will be glad to have me back. I won't have to work down there."

"But the *Tuan's* house is far away," objected the little lad.

"I know the way," said Kondima shortly, "and if you were a smart

111

Jungle Thorn

boy, you would come along with me."

Mookit had risen, but now he sat down again out of sheer astonishment.

"At the *Tuan's* house there are lots of children. They sing and play and laugh. They have lovely food. They have pillows and pajamas, and I am going right now." So saying, she lifted her head proudly, carried the full water bamboos into her hut; then she came out again, closing the door with firm decision. She did not even look at Mookit still sitting where she had left him. Throwing her light scarf over her shoulders, she started up the path toward the top of the hill. She forgot her two dollies snuggled still under the red blanket. She forgot everything but the house of children and the *Tuan*.

Halfway up the hill Mookit overtook her and fell into step. Two little village girls saw the two and ran after them. "Where are you going?" they asked all out of breath.

"We are going to the *Tuan's* house," Mookit answered. "We are tired of working all the time," he snorted in pride; "we go where we will be better treated. "

"My folks are pretty mean to me," said Alijah, "I have to weave baskets and mats all the time, and I have to pound out the rice." She fell into step with the other two. The fourth child said that she, too, was badly treated and felt sure things would be much more pleasant at the *Tuan's* house.

Before they had gone out of the clearing where the village stood, another small boy joined himself to the rebellious travelers; and all five moved into the jungle path that led over the hill and far away.

Kondima cautioned the children about the leeches. "We must go fast," she insisted; "then the leeches will fall where we have been instead of where we are." They hurried so fast that any leech would have had difficulty overtaking them.

Lost And Found

When they came to the valley of the durian trees, there was no fruit because it was not the durian season. However, Kondima seated them all on the grass, and they pretended to feast off the leaves and grass, playing that it was rich and delightful food. With much laughing and eager joy they proceeded on their way.

The children lingered a long time at the top of the mountain where the ocean first became visible. They speculated much on the valley of water, and Kondima gave them such a vivid account of the perils and discomforts of ocean travel that all of them shuddered and hoped they would never have to make a trip by sea.

"Under the water there are great hills and valleys," Kondima informed them. "It is very uncomfortable when the ship passes over them."

The sun was hot as they resumed their journey. It was the busy season in the hills, and few persons were traveling the long trail down to the plain, so the children met with no travelers on the way. Kondima encouraged them with thrilling tales of her marvelous adventures in Singapore and at the house of children. "There will be good food and blankets and pillows and pajamas and toys at the *Tuan's* house." She led the little company on with fine courage.

Early in the afternoon they came to the big rock where the *Tuan* had taken her on his knee on the trip down the mountain. She directed all the children to bathe their feet in the little stream. Then weary and hungry they hastened on their way. "This is where the snake tried to eat the monkeys." Kondima did not need to hurry the little party of drooping children. The thoughts of the great snake lingering in the swamp swept them by the place with winged feet.

The sun was setting when Kondima and her friends emerged from the rubber grove onto the paved highway. No bus was there. Kondima strained her eye as she looked around. A glad cry heartened the group.

"Look, look!" She pointed across a long, low bridge. "See the new houses! That is where the *Tuan* is making his school. Come, we are almost there."

"Who are you?" demanded a tall boy as the children entered the gate close to the nearest of the new buildings. "Who are you, and what do you want?" He eyed the little party of children with a look of mingled interest and disgust.

"We are some of the *Tuan's* children." Kondima looked him straight in the eye. "We have come to live at his house, and we are hungry, and we want to see the *Tuan* and his children."

The schoolboy threw back his tousled head and laughed until he had to lean against the wall of the building. "So you are some of the *Tuan's* children. Ho, ho, ho!" He held his sides with amusement. "I knew the *Tuan* had a lot of children, but I never saw any of them look like you." He laughed with so much scorn in his voice that Kondima stepped boldly up and touched his arm.

"It is true we are dirty and tired, and we don't look so good to you; but the *Tuan* will be glad to see us, for he loves us and wants us to come to his house. I should like to know who you are, and what is your work about the *Tuan's* place."

At this, Majiti, for that was his name, sobered down enough to consider the situation with more composure. "I am come here to go to school," he said with dignity, "and I am left to watch this house. I sleep here at night, and I help with the buildings in the daytime." He hesitated, evidently wondering why he had to give an account of himself to this small girl.

"The *Tuan* is not here," he added. "He went into the city this afternoon and took the family with him. They have not yet returned."

Over the little group fell a shadow that had nothing to do with the approaching darkness. Mookit whispered to Alijah, and all the children squatted down beside the new building to rest their weary legs.

At this moment the sound of a motor car was heard approaching. Two bright headlights turned in at the gate, and the car came to a stop in front of the building. All the children sprang to their feet.

"*Tuan*," Majiti called as he advanced to the side of the car, "here are five children come from the mountains just now. They say they belong to you and have come to live at your house." He indicated the forlorn group with a disdainful wave of his hand.

The *Tuan* looked out into the twilight and saw the five little folk standing in a row. He said not a word, but leaned on the steering wheel and laughed until the surrounding forest resounded again and again. All hearts grew lighter. If the *Tuan* could laugh like that, he could not be too displeased at their coming. They drew a little nearer the car.

"What shall we do with them, *Tuan*?" Majiti inquired in a voice of disgust.

Tuan went off into another fit of uncontrollable laughter, at which the children advanced another step nearer the car.

"Look, Majiti," *Tuan* finally said when he could catch his voice again, "of course they have run away and they will have to be sent

Jungle Thorn

home; but we must feed them and make them happy till their parents arrive. Come over to my house. I will give you plenty of rice and fish and vegetables so you can cook them a good meal. I will take them to the river to get them cleaned up, and then we will find blankets and mosquito curtains for them."

No merrier party ever had a swim in the old Tuaran River. The *Tuan* played with them for an hour. The moon was full, and the water in the river was refreshing. When they returned from their bath, a feast was spread the like of which none of them had seen or tasted before— that is, none but Kondima.

"You see?" Kondima nudged Mookit who was stuffing his mouth like one of Gooloon's pigs. "You see? We are all his children. Have we not eaten his rice in his house?"

The *Tuan* had risen from his place among them and was saying something important. He looked about kindly on them all. The feeble light of the lantern cast dark shadows on his thin face.

"I am very happy to have a visit from you little ones"—he opened both arms wide to all five—" but we are not quite ready to treat you as you should be treated. We do not yet have a proper place for you to live." He swept his hand toward the mountains. "All you mountain children need to go to a school, and we are building a school here. As soon as it is done, I will come to your village and bring you. Then we will learn many wonderful things and have a good time together. Tonight you must stay with us, but in the morning I will take you home to your village, and I will tell your parents about the new school."

A sigh arose from the group, but the littlest boy had already fallen asleep; and the *Tuan* quickly put them away for the night. The whole family retired to rest. Kondima dropped at once into deep sleep, but shortly after midnight she woke suddenly. She crept out of the mosquito curtain and looked out the small loft window. A party of men

Lost And Found

was approaching the buildings. They carried torches in their hands, and Kondima could distinguish by the flickering light the face of her own father and Mookit's father and Alijah's father—all the fathers were there. They stood shouting before the gate.

"We ask shelter for the night." They raised their discouraged voices higher. The *Tuan's* head appeared in the window.

"We seek our children. They are lost; we have hunted them all the night, and we ask your help to find them. Have pity on us! "

Kondima's heart did a quick somersault. She had not realized the grief it would bring to her beloved father for her to be lost.

"Your children are here," *Tuan's* assuring voice rang out in the darkness. "They are all safe and well taken care of."

"Thank God!" said all five in one breath. "The Lord is merciful!" Then *Tuan* came out and brought the men into his house and made them comfortable for the rest of the night.

Late next morning a party of ten persons set off for the Durian village laden with good things and fully instructed about the new school. The boys and girls went with light hearts. The rugged journey seemed short and easy, for they all were the *Tuan's* children now.

Kondima tries to keep the dirty pigs away from their home and out of the garden.

Chapter Twelve

The Pigs That Preached
The Gospel

"Love is remembered, in heaven remembered,
Love shall be crowned when the victory is won;
Good cannot perish, bright ages shall cherish
Holy remembrance of what love has done."

WHAT a filthy place this is! It was Teacher *Daud* speaking. He had just come to the spring to take his morning wash. At his approach a whole herd of pigs had slithered out of the mud and scampered down the hill. "Something must be done about it. It is not right for Christian people to have to put up with such dirty animals."

Kondima, who was following him down to the spring with her cake of yellow soap and her bundle of dirty clothes, held her nose and made a snorting exclamation of disgust. "Are there pigs in other countries?" she asked the young teacher.

"Yes, I suppose there are," he answered, "but I'm sure they are not allowed to run everywhere and dirty everything people have to live with."

"I have heard that none of the people who worship God keep pigs." Kondima spread her washing on the rock and waited patiently

Jungle Thorn

for the water to settle.

"That is not entirely true," Teacher *Daud* replied as he also waited. "You see, many millions of people are Mohammedans, and they all hate pigs. No pigs are allowed in any of their villages, so people have got the idea that all worshipers of God hate pigs."

"Well, I hate them." Kondima began to wash. "I wonder if all the Christian people would help if we built a fence that would keep them out of our side of the village."

"That's a good idea, child." *Daud* scratched his head. "Of course, we couldn't fence the spring, but it would keep them out of our gardens and away from our homes."

The good idea about the fence might have waited for many a day to be carried out, but something else happened that very day to arouse the anger of the village people to fever heat. Gooloon's house stood near to the house of Kondima's father. In fact, those two houses marked a rough boundary line between the heathen and the Christian sides of the village. Since Gooloon had more pigs than anyone else, they were always swarming around the hut of Kondima.

"Take Bani down and let him play on the grass with his motor cars," Mother said to Chaya. "He makes so much noise the baby won't go to sleep."

Chaya picked up her brother and carried him down to a small patch of grass under the durian tree.

Just at that moment Kondima came down the ladder with a small bag of something in her hand.

"What is it, Kondima?" Chaya was up in a minute, and her brown eyes grew big with surprise as she saw her little sister untie her handkerchief and empty out a quantity of brown seed.

"What are they?" Mookit came up to see, and Alijah looked out the window of her hut, then scurried down the ladder.

The Pigs That Preached The Gospel

"These are apple seeds,'" she explained to the wondering children. Then she ran back into the house to bring out a picture book with a picture of a large, round red fruit. "I had one of them every day in the hospital, and I saved all the seeds. I am going to plant them, and maybe they will grow up and have apples on them." Kondima danced with excitement. She tied the seeds in the handkerchief again. "I will plant them when we can keep the pigs away."

While the children had been absorbed in the wonderful apple seeds, Baby Bani had gone on an expedition of his own. He had left the spot of green grass and was now crawling in the mud under Kokit's house. An old sow with a litter of young pigs was there also, and she resented this small intruder. She rushed at him with a heavy grunt, knocking him over on his back and fastening her teeth in one fat leg. Baby Bani yelled. Such screams and howls issued from under the house that people came running from all directions. Bani was rescued by Chaya and carried to the spring, where his wound was washed, and he was given some first-aid treatment by Teacher *Daud*; but Kondima, Mookit, and Alijah did not stop screaming. Some kind of terror seemed to have laid hold on them. In all their lives they had never known a pig to bite anyone before. They knew that the pigs were dirty and smelly and a dreadful nuisance; but the fact that one of them would bite a baby, their own Baby Bani, filled the children with such terror that they gave way to uncontrolled fright.

That evening when Father returned from the rice fields, he was told the whole story. He examined his little son's leg and found it swollen and red from the pig bite. His anger rose and, putting the child in the mother's arms, he went down the ladder and over to Teacher *Daud's* house.

"Is there nothing to be done about these pigs?" His eyes flashed. Kondima had followed him, fairly bursting with rage herself.

Jungle Thorn

"I think the time has come for all the Christian men in this village to make a protest to the government," Teacher *Daud* exclaimed. "And the time has come for us to get together and build a stout fence around our houses."

In the excitement of the moment several strong men volunteered. Strong stakes were cut and driven deeply into the earth. Then heavy strands of rattan were woven between them to make a stout fence. Teacher *Daud* encouraged them to keep at the work, and in a few days the barrier was complete, and also the protest had been sent to the government.

Weeks went by. It had been nearly four months since Kondima had returned to the village. The pigtight fence had worked very well. A few weak places had been revealed from time to time, but willing hands always laid hold and built a stronger barrier than before. The two portions of the village began to assume quite a different appearance. All the Christian people had planted gardens about their houses. *Tuan* had furnished flower seeds, and some vegetable seeds had been gotten from the Chinese gardeners down in the far valley. Kondima had even planted some of her apple seeds, and they had grown a few beautiful leaves. These were the pride of the small folk in the village. Kondima and Chaya watched over them every hour.

The green grass had also sprung up around the huts of the Christian villagers, but the pig-infested portion of the village presented a most disgusting appearance. It came about that when any of the heathen women wanted to sit outside in the sun to weave or sew, they always came over the fence and sat down where the ground was clean.

"*Tuan* is coming! *Tuan* is coming!" Mookit shouted the glad news through the village. Sure enough, a group of travelers was just emerging from the jungle in the dusk of evening. It was already too dark to see clearly who was coming.

The Pigs That Preached The Gospel

"It is not our *Tuan*." Kondima watched the party draw near. "I never saw this *Tuan* before."

Teacher *Daud* went out to meet the newcomers and invited them to his neat cottage, where they entered with grateful expressions of thanks.

"It is the government *Tuan*," Father explained to his family a few minutes later. "He has come to answer our complaint about the pigs." Father put on his best shirt, went down the ladder and over to *Daud's* house.

"Come, Chaya, let us hide in *Daud's* kitchen; then we can see and hear what goes on. "Kondima drew her sister with her, and the two girls squatted in the darkness just inside the kitchen door. They could hear fairly well but could not be easily seen.

"Of course, you know that the government allows all people to keep whatever animals they require for the use of their households." It was the new *Tuan* speaking, the government *Tuan*. He was a young man with kind blue eyes. "We can't prohibit anyone from keeping pigs." He shifted his tired legs a little. "It seems rather unreasonable for you," addressing *Daud*, "to request that a government official should come here and discuss it with you."

Teacher *Daud* spoke very gently. "We do not wish to be unkind to our neighbors," he began. "We only wish to live in peace and quietness and have our gardens and our houses clean, and we like to have proper places for our children to play where the pigs will not molest them."

Then Father spoke up and told how the pig had bitten Baby Bani. Some of the other villagers had something to say also. The heathen men were all arguing for the pigs. Finally the government *Tuan* said he was very tired, and they would discuss it some more in the morning when he had time to talk more fully about it.

Kondima was at the spring early in the morning; so were *Daud*

Jungle Thorn

and several others, including the visitors. As usual the pigs had been there first. Everyone had to wait for the fouled water to settle before they could have their morning wash.

"I say, my friend, these pigs are dirty things." It was the government *Tuan* speaking. Teacher *Daud* said nothing.

"Is this the Christian side of the village?" asked the official as he climbed the stile over the fence to get back to Teacher *Daud's* house.

"We have built a fence around our homes," said *Daud*, watching with interest the exploring eyes of the *Tuan* as he stood on the top of the stile and looked first at one section of the village and then at the other.

"What are these?" he asked of Kondima who was eagerly watching every move and listening to every word. "What are these plants? They look like young apple trees."

"Yes, yes," Kondima said as she looked up into his face. "They are my apple trees." She swept her hand over them proudly. "These are the flowers of Chaya and Mookit." She indicated a bed of marigolds and zinnias in full bloom.

"Now exactly what do you want done about these pigs?" the government official asked of Teacher *Daud* when they reached his house.

"We want the pigs to be fenced in proper pens, or else we want them to be gotten rid of," *Daud* answered. "Of course, the best thing would be if the heathen people could be persuaded to get rid of them themselves. Could you not make them a good speech of pleasant words which would cause their hearts to turn against the pigs?" *Daud* looked appealingly at the white man.

The government *Tuan* laughed. "I will do my best; please call all the village fathers together and give me a chance."

Daud took a buffalo horn from the wall of his cottage and blew a long blast on it. It was the signal for assembly. It was used to call

The Pigs That Preached The Gospel

the people to worship and to council. It was not many minutes until the people could be seen moving toward the teacher's hut from all directions.

"My friends," the official began, "I had not realized the beauty of your village until this morning. You remember it was nearly dark when I came in last night. This morning I have had time to look around and see what a lovely spot it is. The government is interested in having some of these villages in beautiful locations such as this one to be developed into places which may be visited by strangers to our country and which will give them a good impression of the people and their habits of living." He looked round on everyone with a disarming smile. "Of course, I realize that it is your privilege to keep your pigs as long as they are fenced in yards where they will not annoy your neighbors; but since you already have so many beautiful gardens here and such a good start toward making your village one of the finest in the mountains, the government would count it a great favor if you would sell off your pigs and devote yourselves to making the whole village like this garden here." He indicated the plot belonging to Kondima's father. "I don't pay too much attention to religion, but I must say your pigs have preached the strongest sermon to me I have heard in many a day."

After the government *Tuan* had gone, there was much discussion. *Daud* spent days visiting back and forth among his flock, as well as among the heathen people. Finally the day was set by the heathen people on which they declared a great feast.

Kondima never forgot that day. Early in the morning the killing of pigs began. Then great preparation for feasting began among all the heathen villagers.

"We may as well eat them all up and be done with them," said Gooloon.

Jungle Thorn

After the pigs were all gone, the fence was taken down. The flowers and vegetables were shared by all, and there was now no barrier to Gooloon's acceptance of the Jesus teaching.

"Come to my house, Teacher," Gooloon said as he appeared at *Daud's* hut early one morning, his face wreathed in smiles. "I want you to pray to the God in heaven and ask His blessing on us all. My wife gave birth to a son last night."

Kondima, listening from her window, rejoiced. "The pigs and the devils are being driven out of Durian village," she remarked to Chaya. "Come, let us go and see the new baby."

We invite you to view the complete
selection of titles we publish at:

www.TEACHServices.com

Scan with your mobile
device to go directly
to our website.

Please write or email us your praises, reactions, or
thoughts about this or any other book we publish at:

TEACH Services, Inc.
PUBLISHING

www.TEACHServices.com • (800) 367-1844

P.O. Box 954
Ringgold, GA 30736

info@TEACHServices.com

TEACH Services, Inc., titles may be purchased in bulk for
educational, business, fund-raising, or sales promotional use.
For information, please e-mail:

BulkSales@TEACHServices.com

Finally, if you are interested in seeing
your own book in print, please contact us at

publishing@TEACHServices.com

We would be happy to review your manuscript for free.

d

9 781572 581579